What business leaders are saying about Marketing Masterplan

"Planning your marketing strategy shouldn't be complicated - and thanks to Simon, this book makes it easier and enjoyable!"

"What a book this is! Simon has knocked it out of the park with his Marketing Masterplan. A world of information to kick your marketing into high gear, complete with exercises, activities, and hot tips to really drive home the concepts!"

"It's a great book! Such simple, understandable and practical advice that will help SMEs enormously"

"I'm really impressed with the content, layout and just how friendly Marketing Masterplan is. One of those books that you can go to when you need to work something out or get a practical solution. It will be a great help to sole traders, SMEs and even the corporates could learn something!! Well worth a copy on your bookshelf!"

"If someone had previously asked me what marketing was, I would have said 'flashy websites and leaflets'. Then I read the Marketing Masterplan and soon began to understand the importance of strategy - the journey you want your customers to experience and how you position your business as a living breathing entity, something I would never have been able to do myself."

Many thanks to my good friend and colleague - Helen Shinner, for helping me make this book become a reality.

Copyright © 2022 by Simon Clayton, Marketing Skills Academy.

All rights reserved. No part of this publication may be reproduced, distributed, or transmitted in any form or by any means, including photocopying, recording, or other electronic or mechanical methods, without the prior written permission of the publisher, except in the case of brief quotations embodied in critical reviews and certain other noncommercial uses permitted by copyright law. For permission requests, please email the publisher, addressed "Attention: Permissions Coordinator," to simon@marketingskillsacademy.co.uk or tel: 01642 688678.

Marketing Skills Academy is a registered trading name for Elevation Marketing Limited. Registered in England & Wales No. 9163358.

Ordering Information: Quantity sales - special discounts are available on quantity purchases by corporations, associations, and others. For details, contact the publisher at the address above. Printed in the United Kingdom.

Welcome

You're here because you want to achieve success in your business.

Many want the same, but you have one key difference –
you've taken action to make it happen.

This course is for those who *know* their business has potential, and
need guidance on marketing – finding opportunities, maximising
them and turning them into sales.

In this book you will learn:

- Who and where your most profitable customers are

- How to attract, engage and communicate with them

- What differentiates your business from your competitors

- How to build brand visibility and generate new sales leads

- The conversion formula used to turn a cold prospect into a hot lead

- What makes customers keep coming back time and time again

Marketing Skills Academy has worked with a wide range of organisations over the last 25 years, from SMEs to global brands. We only work with business people who are **motivated, work hard and are hungry for success**. It will take time and commitment but you **WILL** see a difference.

How does the book work?
We've broken the marketing process down into 6 sections:

- **PURPOSE** – do you know why your business exists?

- **INTELLIGENCE** – do you understand your customer and their motivations to purchase?

- **PROPOSITION** – why do customers buy from you? Is your USP clear in your key messages?

- **TOOLS** – can you identify the right marketing tools and kick out the ones that are costing you money?

- **CONVERSION** – are you a pro at turning interested customers into paying customers?

- **RESULTS** – can you measure your marketing activity and refine it to become even more effective?

In each section you'll find information on marketing best practice and how to apply it to your business. We've included activities to focus your strategy and make sure you're getting the most out of the content.

This book has been designed so you can dip back in to any of the six sections at any time. And we highly recommend you do so – you'll be surprised how much changes as your business grows.

Ready to grow your business?

Let's dive in...

Simon Clayton

Simon Clayton
Founder of Marketing Skills Academy

01
Purpose

01 Purpose
02 Intelligence
03 Proposition
04 Tools
05 Conversion
06 Results

01

Purpose

"The reason for which something is done or created or for which something exists."

Oxford Dictionary, 2018

01 Purpose
02 Intelligence
03 Proposition
04 Tools
05 Conversion
06 Results

01

Purpose

What is your purpose?

So here we begin... at the very start of this exciting journey together. Before we dive into creating your marketing masterplan, we first need to answer four important questions regarding your business's 'purpose':

1. **WHY does your business exist?** (Purpose of Existence)

2. **WHY should people buy from you?** (Purpose of Reason)

3. **WHY do you need a marketing plan?** (Purpose of Planning)

4. **WHAT do you want your marketing to achieve?** (Purpose of Marketing)

01 Purpose
02 Intelligence
03 Proposition
04 Tools
05 Conversion
06 Results

01
Purpose

Your 'Purpose' Model

+

+

Marketing Objectives

=

PURPOSE

01 Purpose
02 Intelligence
03 Proposition
04 Tools
05 Conversion
06 Results

1.1
Why does your business exist?

Why does your business exist?

REALLY think about why...

What do you believe in? What do you do differently?

It is surprising how many business owners don't actually know why their business exists or what difference their business is going to make to their end user – the customer!

Whilst some may argue,
'Well, isn't this the exciting part of being self employed – not really knowing what's ahead – just keep plugging away, trying to bring the work in and the rewards will follow?'

it can become extremely time and energy consuming (as well as costly), spreading yourself thinly across many different types of customers – trying to please each one who all demand a different relationship with your business.

Hence, we need to first understand what your business is and does.

Then we can define your aims and objectives, which will provide the foundations for your **marketing masterplan.**

01 Purpose
02 Intelligence
03 Proposition
04 Tools
05 Conversion
06 Results

1.1
Why does your business exist?

Values

We begin with your values.

Your 'Purpose of Existence' comes from your values – *the core reasons why a business operates, what it stands for and what drives all other activity.*

A business purpose and values should be central to everything it does – *from its operations to the relationships it builds with customers.*

All businesses should aim to attract customers who share their values.

01 Purpose
02 Intelligence
03 Proposition
04 Tools
05 Conversion
06 Results

1.1

Why does your business exist?

For example: Coca-Cola, the global soft drinks brand, has the following values:

- **Leadership:** The courage to shape a better future.
- **Integrity:** Be real.
- **Collaboration:** Leverage collective genius.
- **Accountability:** If it is to be, it's up to me.
- **Passion:** Committed in heart and mind.
- **Diversity:** As inclusive as our brands.
- **Quality:** What we do, we do well.

For example: BMW, the motor vehicle brand, has the following values:

- **Responsibility:** We take consistent decisions and commit to them personally. This allows us to work freely and more effectively.

- **Appreciation:** We reflect on our actions, respect each other, offer clear feedback and celebrate success.

- **Transparency:** We acknowledge concern and identify inconsistencies in a constructive way. We act with integrity.

- **Trust:** We trust and rely on each other. This is essential if we are to act swiftly and achieve our goals.

- **Openness:** We are excited by change and open to new opportunities. We learn from our mistakes.

01 Purpose
02 Intelligence
03 Proposition
04 Tools
05 Conversion
06 Results

1.1
Why does your business exist?

Let's look at your values right now: can you name them?

1. Honesty
2. Trust
3. Value - Centricity
4. Diversity + Inclusivity
5. Fair(ness)

1.1
Why does your business exist?

Now you've listed your values, would your staff, customers or even suppliers list the same ones?

Ask a few key people what your values are; ideally, they will list the same ones as you no matter what their role or relationship is with your business.

If they name different ones to you, you may need to consider how you communicate your values more effectively.

"If people believe they share values with a company, they will stay loyal to the brand."

Howard Schultz
CEO of Starbucks

01 Purpose
02 Intelligence
03 Proposition
04 Tools
05 Conversion
06 Results

1.1
Why does your business exist?

Summary

You should now understand why your business exists – the purpose of its existence. This includes:

- Your values and what they say about your company
- How your values give your company direction
- The importance of clearly communicating these values to staff and stakeholders

01 Purpose
02 Intelligence
03 Proposition
04 Tools
05 Conversion
06 Results

1.2
Why should people buy from you?

Why should people buy from you?

Picture the scene…

You are attending a business event – an opportunity to network
and meet new contacts – potential customers!

You enter the room, exchanging glances with various people. Some you recognise, others you don't.

Suddenly someone approaches you. You have never met them before – they are friendly, extremely confident and they start talking to you.

They introduce themselves and their business… their unbelievable product/service… their enviable customer base… their amazing sales team…
and this month's 'special offers'.

At this point you're feeling a little overwhelmed – but it continues…

OK, so this sounds like a nightmare scenario (maybe you've experienced it), but it's surprising how many businesses do this – every day – with their marketing.

They constantly push the 'WHAT'.

01 Purpose
02 Intelligence
03 Proposition
04 Tools
05 Conversion
06 Results

1.2
Why should people buy from you?

WHAT!

Are you pushing the 'WHAT'?

- WHAT my business is
- WHAT unbelievable products/services we provide
- WHAT an enviable customer base we have
- WHAT an amazing sales team we have

WHY?

Or do you promote the 'WHY'?

- WHY my business exists
- WHY my product/service will provide unbelievable value for your business
- WHY I know you will be an amazing customer
- WHY I would like to meet with you and learn more about your business

Ask yourself this question:

What are the 'WHY' factors in your business?

1.2
Why should people buy from you?

Why does it work?

As the saying goes, people don't buy what you do, they buy why you do it.

Promoting the WHY works because people buy emotionally and justify logically.

For example, when you're searching for a new car, you may see one that costs very little, has great safety features and low mileage. But it has no 'oomph'. There's just something missing.

Next, you see your dream car. You know this brand, you love their innovations. Wouldn't it be great if you could have one? Well, this one costs more and has fewer features – BUT it does have the safety features and you can pay monthly.

SOLD!

Car manufacturers know that they need to appeal to customers' emotions to make a sale. That's why their TV ads promote beauty, freedom and luxury over more tangible features.

01 Purpose
02 Intelligence
03 Proposition
04 Tools
05 Conversion
06 Results

1.2
Why should people buy from you?

Here are some companies who also promote the WHY and capture this in their slogan:

Have a Break, Have a Kit Kat

Because You're Worth It

The World's Local Bank

01 Purpose
02 Intelligence
03 Proposition
04 Tools
05 Conversion
06 Results

1.2
Why should people buy from you?

Digging deeper: High involvement vs low involvement purchase decisions

The extent to which your purpose impacts your marketing depends on the type of product or service you offer.

Think about a hobby and the last item you purchased for it – a new outfit, a beach holiday, a new car etc. – how long did you spend on that purchase decision? Did you compare brands, benefits, costs and reviews?

Now think about the last time you bought a household cleaning product – how long did you spend on that purchase decision? Maybe you grabbed your usual brand, or the one on offer.

Does your brand require a high or low involvement decision from customers?

Purpose plays a much more important role with **high involvement** decisions.

01 Purpose
02 Intelligence
03 Proposition
04 Tools
05 Conversion
06 Results

1.2
Why should people buy from you?

Determining if your products/services demand high or low involvement purchase decisions

A good way to determine whether your customers use high or low involvement purchase decisions is to look at the typical customer journey.

The customer journey refers to the process someone goes through, from being a member of your target audience to becoming a customer.

During the customer journey, each time the person has any form of contact with your brand, this is known as a 'touchpoint'. Research tells us that the average number of touchpoints someone undergoes before they become a customer is 8.

The plan that follows, is an example of how the customer journey may look to a business to business (B2B) organisation. It shows how many 'touchpoints' it will take before a person converts into a paying customer.

The more targeted touchpoints we can create, the better.

01 Purpose
02 Intelligence
03 Proposition
04 Tools
05 Conversion
06 Results

1.2
Why should people buy from you?

The customer journey for a B2B (business to business) company may look like this:

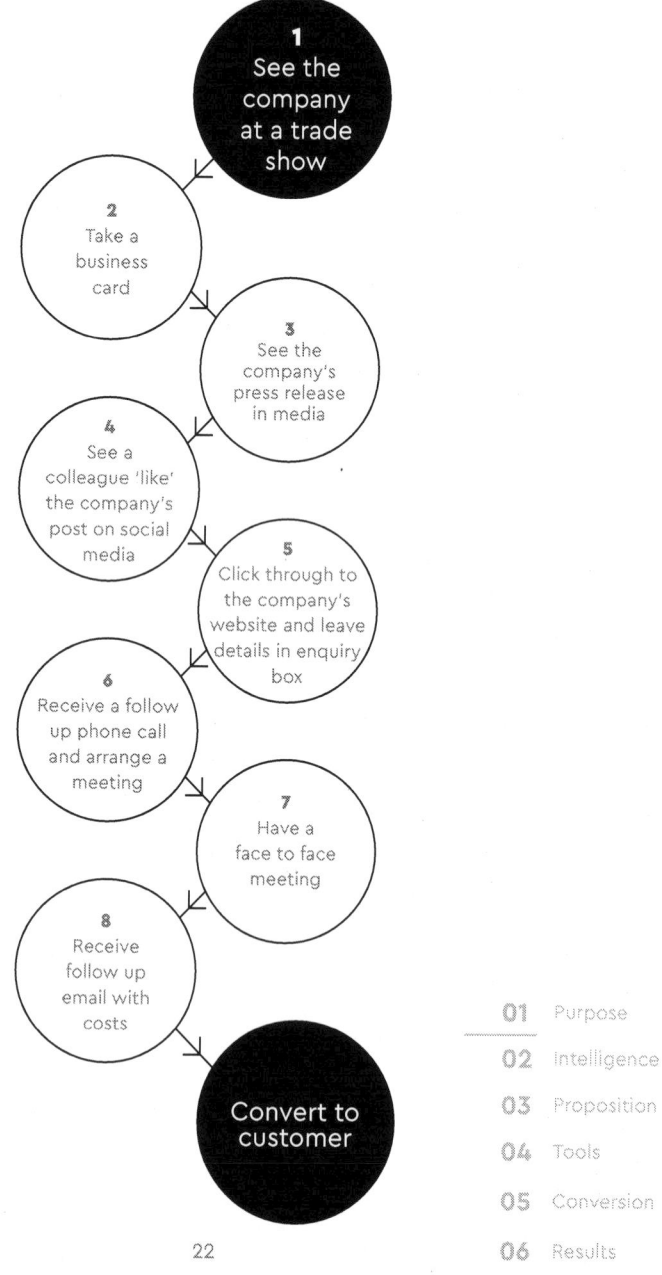

1.2

Why should people buy from you?

Brand touchpoints can include all these!

- Trade shows
- Word of mouth
- Case studies
- Events
- Blog
- Email
- LinkedIn connection requests
- Social media
- Radio
- PR
- TV
- Networking
- Spec sheets
- Interviews
- Sales
- Magazines
- Videos
- Direct marketing
- Technical service
- Printed literature

01 Purpose
02 Intelligence
03 Proposition
04 Tools
05 Conversion
06 Results

1.2
Why should people buy from you?

Activity: How many touchpoints can you name for your average customer? *List them below.*

1	
2	
3	
4	
5	
6	
7	
8	
9	
10	
11	
12	
?	*What's your total number?*

01 Purpose
02 Intelligence
03 Proposition
04 Tools
05 Conversion
06 Results

1.2
Why should people buy from you?

The average number of touchpoints to convert interest into a sale is 8

If yours is below this, and you are making regular sales, your products/services likely involve low involvement decisions.

If your number is higher than 8, your products/services likely involve high involvement decisions.

If you think your sales process should involve high involvement decisions but your number is lower than 8, this could be an indicator that more touchpoints are needed to convert customers.

01 Purpose
02 Intelligence
03 Proposition
04 Tools
05 Conversion
06 Results

1.2

Why should people buy from you?

Summary

You should now understand **why** people buy from you – the purpose of reason.

This includes:

The **why** factors for your company

How pushing the **why** rather than the **what** engages people

Customer **touchpoints** in your own marketing and whether they lend themselves to **high or low** involvement purchase decisions

1.3

Why do you need a marketing plan?

Why do you need a marketing plan?

It's time to set the direction your business is heading in.

The first stage of any marketing planning is to clarify business goals and set clear objectives.

A marketing plan is an action plan, covering the short, intermediate and long-term goals of the business.

It will help you focus and provide direction, by identifying the different ways you can reach, engage and communicate with your customers.

01 Purpose
02 Intelligence
03 Proposition
04 Tools
05 Conversion
06 Results

1.3

Why do you need a marketing plan?

What are business aims?

So let's get started with your business aims.

These are the goals your business wants to achieve in a given time period.

They could be **short term** – *quarterly, half-yearly, annually* or **long term** – *3/5/10 years.*

Common business aims are based around survival, increasing profit, growth and increasing market share.

01 Purpose
02 Intelligence
03 Proposition
04 Tools
05 Conversion
06 Results

1.3
Why do you need a marketing plan?

For example:

- **To increase turnover** – the total amount of money taken by a business in a particular period BEFORE costs and taxes.

- **To increase profitability** – the total amount of money taken by a business in a particular period AFTER costs and taxes.

- **To increase market share** – the portion of a market controlled by a particular company or product.

- **To launch a new business, brand or subsidiary.**

- **To launch a new product (or service)** – often using better processes, skills and technology.

- **To enter a new geographical location.**

1.3
Why do you need a marketing plan?

Big business aims

Google[*]

Google's aim is to organise the world's information and make it universally accessible and useful.

---

facebook[*]

Facebook's aim is to bring the world closer together.

01 Purpose
02 Intelligence
03 Proposition
04 Tools
05 Conversion
06 Results

1.3
Why do you need a marketing plan?

Why set business aims?

Business aims set the direction your company is heading in.

They take into account your mission, vision and values and translate these into a clear destination your business is heading for.

From business aims, measurable marketing objectives can be set.
These are the stepping stones that can be achieved on the way to achieving your overall business aims.

Any leader will tell you that setting a clear direction is imperative to keep your business – and team – on board and ensure everyone is working toward a common goal.

Being aware of the business aims makes day to day decision making easier: the long term plan is laid out, and each smaller decision contributes to the bigger picture.

01 Purpose
02 Intelligence
03 Proposition
04 Tools
05 Conversion
06 Results

1.3
Why do you need a marketing plan?

Setting business aims

Consider your business aims – the fundamental desires that you want your business to achieve to help it grow.

For example, *'the aim for our business is to become the leading national manufacturer of industrial components for widget machines'.*

This statement does not say specifically how your company can reach its goal, but it does serve an important purpose.

Setting aims helps define the direction that a business will take.

01 Purpose
02 Intelligence
03 Proposition
04 Tools
05 Conversion
06 Results

1.3
Why do you need a marketing plan?

Activity: What are your business aims?

Think about the fundamental desires you have for your business and list them below:

SHORT TERM 1-6 MONTHS

1.
2.
3.
4.
5.

MEDIUM TERM 6-12 MONTHS

1.
2.
3.
4.
5.

LONG TERM 1/3/5 YEARS

1.
2.
3.
4.
5.

01 Purpose
02 Intelligence
03 Proposition
04 Tools
05 Conversion
06 Results

1.3

Why do you need a marketing plan?

Summary

You should now understand why you need a marketing plan – the purpose of planning. This includes:

- ✓ Why your business needs to set goals
- ✓ How to clearly define what you want
- ✓ What your short, medium and long term aims are

01 Purpose
02 Intelligence
03 Proposition
04 Tools
05 Conversion
06 Results

1.4
What do you want your marketing to achieve?

What do you want your marketing to achieve?

The purpose of marketing is to plan the path your business will take to reach its destination and achieve its business aims.

1.4
What do you want your marketing to achieve?

Marketing objectives

Your marketing objectives should aim to set out the actions needed to reach your business aims. The terms objectives and aims are often used interchangeably, but **each serves a different purpose and are used at different stages of the marketing planning process.**

The success or failure of a strategy is very much defined by setting measurable objectives and regularly tracking your results.

Typical marketing objectives may focus on topics such as:

- Increase brand awareness to a specific audience
- Generate sales leads from new customers
- Communicate more effectively with existing customers
- Increase market share within a specific industry sector

01 Purpose
02 Intelligence
03 Proposition
04 Tools
05 Conversion
06 Results

1.4
What do you want your marketing to achieve?

SMART Objectives

The simplest way to set your marketing objectives is to follow the SMART approach.

S = Specific

Objectives must have a specific outcome:

- *What exactly do I want to achieve?*
- *Where do I want to achieve it?*
- *How do I want to achieve it?*
- *When do I want to achieve it?*

Try to be as specific as possible, as this will help you make more guided judgements and keep you focused on the end result.

1.4
What do you want your marketing to achieve?

M = Measurable

Apply a set of quantifiable metrics to track and evaluate the success of the objective:

- *What does the end result look like?*
- *How do I know if I'm making progress?*
- *And, how do I know when I get there?*

By clearly defining the physical changes for when your reach your objectives, you will make them clearer and easier to reach.

01 Purpose
02 Intelligence
03 Proposition
04 Tools
05 Conversion
06 Results

1.4
What do you want your marketing to achieve?

A = Attainable

Objectives must have achievable outcomes to reach your overall goals:

- *How achievable are your objectives?*
- *How much effort is required?*

You must consider whether the amount of effort, time and resources you will invest will provide the outcome you desire – physically, emotionally and financially.

1.4
What do you want your marketing to achieve?

R = Relevant

Also known as realistic. Make sure the resources are available to achieve the objective i.e. people, funds, equipment, materials and time.

- *Why do you want to reach these objectives?*
- *How relevant are they to you, your business and your desired future?*

Matching your strengths, skills and experience is important when considering how relevant your objectives are.

01 Purpose
02 Intelligence
03 Proposition
04 Tools
05 Conversion
06 Results

1.4
What do you want your marketing to achieve?

T = Timely

What is the specific timeframe to reach your objectives
– days, weeks, months or even years?

- **How much time do you need?**
- **Do you have a timeline for reaching these objectives?**

Time is an essential factor when planning objectives –

"time is money", as the saying goes. Make sure you plan for everything you do and keep the timeline realistic and flexible, that way you can keep your energy and morale high.

01 Purpose
02 Intelligence
03 Proposition
04 Tools
05 Conversion
06 Results

1.4
What do you want your marketing to achieve?

Examples of SMART objectives:

- To increase the average order amount by £60 during the Christmas period, from 1st November to 24th December

- To have at least 60% of previous customers make a repeat purchase in the next 12 months.

- To increase revenue across the whole business by at least 20% per year for the next 3 years.

1.4
What do you want your marketing to achieve?

Activity: Make your own SMART objectives

It's time to work the SMART magic on your own organisation. Complete the template, on the next page, with your own objectives.

01 Purpose
02 Intelligence
03 Proposition
04 Tools
05 Conversion
06 Results

1.4

What do you want your marketing to achieve?

SETTING SMART OBJECTS			
	OBJECTIVE 1	**OBJECTIVE 2**	**OBJECTIVE 3**
SPECIFIC			
What do I actually want to achieve?			
Where do I want to achieve it?			
How do I want to achieve it?			
When do I want to achieve it?			
MEASURABLE			
What does the end result look like?			
How do I know if I'm making progress?			
What specific elements will I measure?			
How will I know when I get there?			

01 Purpose
02 Intelligence
03 Proposition
04 Tools
05 Conversion
06 Results

1.4

What do you want your marketing to achieve?

	OBJECTIVE 1	OBJECTIVE 2	OBJECTIVE 3
ATTAINABLE			
What reasons are there for me achieving this objective?			
How much effort is required?			
RELEVANT			
Why do I want to reach this objective?			
What impact will it have on my business?			
How relevant is it to me; my business; my future aspirations?			
TIMELY			
How much time is required to achieve this objective?			
What is the timeline for reaching this objective – days, weeks, months, years?			

01 Purpose
02 Intelligence
03 Proposition
04 Tools
05 Conversion
06 Results

1.4
What do you want your marketing to achieve?

Summary

You should now understand what you want your marketing to achieve.

This includes:

- ✓ How marketing objectives feed in to your business aims
- ✓ How your objectives will help you track your results
- ✓ The importance of setting **SMART** objectives

01 Purpose
02 Intelligence
03 Proposition
04 Tools
05 Conversion
06 Results

1.5
ACTION TIME!

ACTION TIME!
Summary

Throughout this section we have looked at **purpose**, whilst setting the groundwork for your marketing plan.

We've explored the key components that will set your direction and keep you on track, and discussed why these are important.

Everything in this section serves to create a solid foundation from which your marketing masterplan can be based.

Try not to think of this section as a one-off exercise – revisit it often to use it as a benchmark for what you want to achieve and to measure your ongoing activity against your original business aims and marketing objectives.

01 Purpose
02 Intelligence
03 Proposition
04 Tools
05 Conversion
06 Results

1.5
ACTION TIME!

Tip: think critically

Sometimes it's easy to focus on the day to day running of your business and lose sight of how customers view the business.

Try to always think critically and ask questions to keep on track.

In particular, what would a customer think of your plans?

What would a competitor think of them?

Your knowledge of the market and the customer is a huge asset that can be used to fault find and resolve potential problems before they arise.

01 Purpose
02 Intelligence
03 Proposition
04 Tools
05 Conversion
06 Results

1.5

ACTION TIME!

Taking your learning forward

- Ensure your business values are clearly communicated to everyone within your organisation, from Directors to front line staff.

- Ask a sample of people in your target market how they perceive your business – if it doesn't match the image you want to portray, it may be an indication of unclear or inconsistent communications.

- Reinforce to your staff the importance making your organisation's activities consistent with the business aims and marketing objectives. Every decision should contribute to overall aims.

- Provide clear direction and a focus for all marketing decision-making and effort. This includes establishing priorities and providing physical and financial resources.

- Motivate staff and increase their drive to achieve goals (are they aware of the aims and objectives, and are they encouraged to take action to achieve these?). Provide incentives as needed.

- Use the activities completed in this section as a benchmark against which you can measure success and review plans as necessary.

01 Purpose
02 Intelligence
03 Proposition
04 Tools
05 Conversion
06 Results

1.5
───
ACTION TIME!

Implementing these Principles

As well as applying the theory and practical exercises to your own business, there are other ways to take your learning forward in your organisation.

The following checklist provides further points to consider that will consolidate the learning in this section.

01 Purpose
02 Intelligence
03 Proposition
04 Tools
05 Conversion
06 Results

1.5
ACTION TIME!

Checklist

- I understand my business's purpose and the role it plays in the marketplace.

- My values align with my target customers'.

- I have set clear business aims that will help achieve my company mission.

- The marketing objectives I've set meet every element of SMART and contribute to achieving the overall business aims.

- Everyone in my organisation is aware of these aims and objectives, and their role in achieving them.

01 Purpose
02 Intelligence
03 Proposition
04 Tools
05 Conversion
06 Results

02

Intelligence

02
Intelligence

"If you do not know where you come from, then you don't know where you are, and if you don't know where you are, then you don't know where you're going. And if you don't know where you're going, you're probably going wrong."

Sir Terry Pratchett, Author

01	Purpose
02	Intelligence
03	Proposition
04	Tools
05	Conversion
06	Results

02

Intelligence

Intelligence

You know your business and its purpose; now it's time to gather intelligence and use it to analyse the market you're operating in.

Carrying out research isn't the most thrilling part of business, but spend some time getting this right now and it will put you miles ahead in the long run.

Be the tortoise, not the hare.

02
Intelligence

Questions

In this section we'll look at:

1	The difference between customers and consumers?

2	How do customer personas give us insight?

3	What can you learn from your competitors?

4	What does your existing data tell you?

5	What's your SWOT (Strengths, Weaknesses, Opportunities and Threats)?

01 Purpose
02 Intelligence
03 Proposition
04 Tools
05 Conversion
06 Results

2.0

Intelligence

Your 'Intelligence' Model

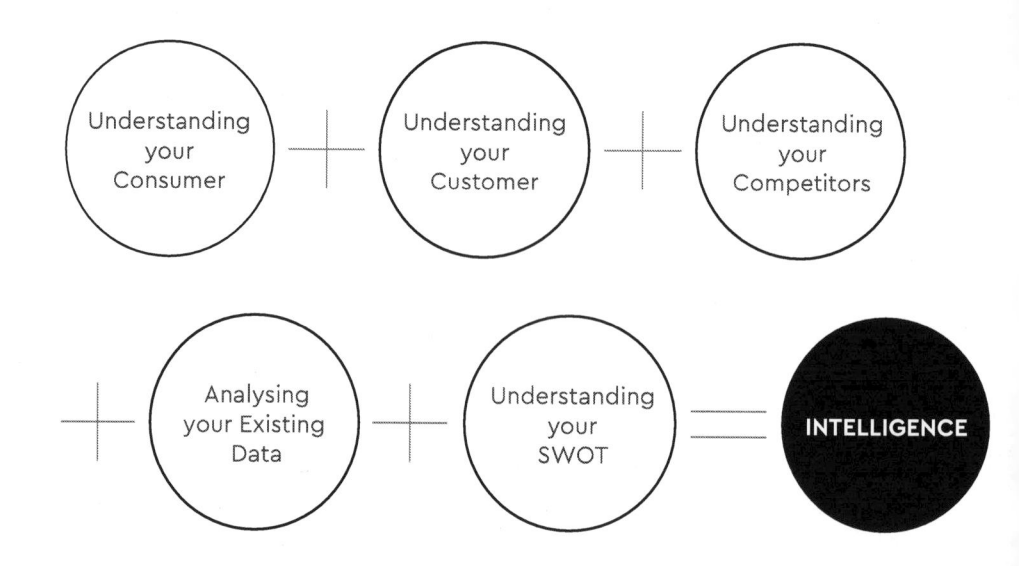

Understanding your Consumer + Understanding your Customer + Understanding your Competitors

+ Analysing your Existing Data + Understanding your SWOT = **INTELLIGENCE**

01 Purpose
02 Intelligence
03 Proposition
04 Tools
05 Conversion
06 Results

2.1
Understanding Consumers and Customers

Understanding Consumers and Customers

Before we dive in, let's distinguish between your customers and your consumers. These terms are often used interchangeably, but for this section it's essential to differentiate between the two.

A **customer** is the person who physically **buys and pays for** your product or service.

A **consumer** is the person who **uses** your product or service.

2.1
Understanding Consumers and Customers

For example:

Jeff's company makes luxury toiletries.
He sells them in bulk to hotels across the UK.

The hotels are his **customers**, but they are not the **consumer**.

The **consumers** are the hotel guests who use the products.

Jeff's customers have very different needs and wants to his consumers. The customers want the product to look nice on the shelf, they want miniature sizes to reduce wastage and they want to know they're getting a good price for buying in bulk. Jeff's consumers want the toiletries to look nice and perform well – they want to feel like they have received a treat and had an experience they wouldn't have at home.

Customers and consumers are often the same person, but not always.

When it comes to your marketing plan, the distinction is important because it raises the question...

2.1
Understanding Consumers and Customers

Who should I target my marketing at - the *customer* or *consumer*?

It can be easy to focus on either the customer or consumer, but the most successful companies will consider both.

This is why it's essential to understand the **needs** and **wants** of both your customers and consumers. Both groups affect the level of demand that exists for your products or services.

By adapting and tailoring your marketing plan to accommodate both, you are expanding your reach and increasing the likelihood of converting your target audience into paying customers.

01 Purpose
02 Intelligence
03 Proposition
04 Tools
05 Conversion
06 Results

2.1
Understanding Consumers and Customers

Activity: Customers, consumers and your marketing plan

Look at the following table to see how Jeff's company considers his customers and consumers, and the consequences for his marketing plan.

Then use the blank template to do the same for your business.

2.1

Understanding Consumers and Customers

Activity:

Jeff's company	Customer	Consumer
Who are they?	Hotel chains, independent hotels	Hotel guests
What's important to them when considering your products/services?	• Attractive packaging • Low unit price • Miniature sizes to reduce wastage • Suppliers used must be environmentally friendly	• Attractive packaging – luxury feel • Nice scent • Good performance – want the products to do their job well
What are the key messages to communicate to each group?	• Show visuals of luxury style packaging • Bulk buy and repeat order discounts available • Multiple sizes available • Promote commitment to reducing carbon footprint	• Luxury style packaging and branding • Carefully considered messaging such as 'treat yourself', 'indulgent' or 'spa experience' • Descriptive language around scents and ingredients used
Where would these messages be communicated?	In all marketing and communications	On pack only

01 Purpose
02 Intelligence
03 Proposition
04 Tools
05 Conversion
06 Results

2.1
Understanding Consumers and Customers

Activity: Your turn

Your company	Customer	Consumer
Who are they?		
What's important to them when considering your products/services?		
What are the key messages to communicate to each group?		
Where would these messages be communicated?		

01 Purpose
02 Intelligence
03 Proposition
04 Tools
05 Conversion
06 Results

2.1

Understanding Consumers and Customers

Summary

You should now understand the difference between customers and consumers. This includes:

1	Why it's important to distinguish between the two groups
2	What each group wants and needs
3	The consequences for your marketing plan

01 Purpose
02 Intelligence
03 Proposition
04 Tools
05 Conversion
06 Results

2.2

Understanding your Customer: Customer Personas

Understanding your Customer: Customer Personas

> Defining who your potential customers are and what motivates them to make a purchase gives you the power to convert them into paying customers.

2.2

Understanding your Customer: Customer Personas

How to define your target audiences

You may think you already know your customers – both existing and potential new ones – yet there's very often a gap between the basics you already know, and the behaviours and preferences that are key to reaching your target market **and selling to them**. Having a well-defined target market is crucial to the success of any marketing activity.

One of the most effective ways to achieve this is to create customer personas, which are a physical and visual representation of your ideal buyer – based on your knowledge and experience of your existing customer base.

Ideally, a customer persona should enable you to develop an understanding of how your existing and potential new customers make assumptions **before purchase**; define reasons **to purchase**; and how they feel and react **after purchase**.

01 Purpose
02 Intelligence
03 Proposition
04 Tools
05 Conversion
06 Results

2.2

Understanding your Customer: Customer Personas

How to define your target audiences

By creating customer personas, you can then focus your marketing efforts on a more concentrated group of people, enabling you to target smaller, niche markets.

It will allow you to create content and marketing messages that appeals directly to your target audience.

More importantly, if it's a sector you have knowledge and commercial experience in, you can empathise and adapt more quickly, as well as operate with authority and confidence.

This type of target marketing will allow you to focus your marketing budget and brand message on specific businesses that are more likely to buy from you.

It is also a much more affordable, efficient, and effective way to reach potential clients and generate new business leads.

01 Purpose
02 Intelligence
03 Proposition
04 Tools
05 Conversion
06 Results

2.2

Understanding your Customer: Customer Personas

What are pain points?

Part of defining the customer persona involves identifying 'pain points'.

These are problems or challenges that the customer experiences that may affect their buying decisions. Once you understand what pain points are, you can work out your response and increase the likelihood of the customer buying from your business.

For example, many business leaders would benefit from coaching but are simply too busy for face-to-face sessions.

Marketing Skills Academy has considered this and provided a solution – online resources that can be accessed anytime, as well as out of hours sessions that can be done via Skype or telephone.

It sounds simple, but before this was an option many potential customers simply would not have been able to buy from us.

01 Purpose
02 Intelligence
03 Proposition
04 Tools
05 Conversion
06 Results

2.2

Understanding your Customer: Customer Personas

Top tip

*If you found in the previous section that **your consumers are different to your customers**, throughout this section it will be **extremely useful** to define them in addition to your customers.*

2.2

Understanding your Customer: Customer Personas

Activity: Create your customer personas

The chances are, you'll have a wide variety of people buying from you.

Use the following table as a template to create a customer persona for each type of customer (and consumer).

01 Purpose
02 Intelligence
03 Proposition
04 Tools
05 Conversion
06 Results

2.2

Understanding your Customer: Customer Personas

DEVELOPING CUSTOMER PERSONAS		EXAMPLE: *JEFF'S COMPANY*
Persona Name: A fictional name for this customer persona group		Hotel chains
DEMOGRAPHICS		
Who are they? (Individual / organisation / couple / group)		Large hotel chains operating in the UK. We will be speaking to Purchasing Managers.
What is their gender? (Male or female)		Either
How old are they? Age bracket (16-24; 25-34; 35-49; 50-64; 65+)		Typically 30-50
What is their status / title? (Owner / MD, Director, Manager, Self-Employed, Retired...)		Manager – has responsibility for purchase decisions
INTERESTS		
What are their interests? (Sport, lifestyle, leisure, hobbies...)		They think on behalf of their hotel chain which may be professional/quirky/fun
What are their likes and dislikes?		Like to save their company money, enjoy sourcing new products, like receiving free samples. Dislike time consuming purchases, too much paperwork.
MEDIA CONSUMPTION		
What is their media consumption? (Social media, websites, print, TV, radio)		They are often found on LinkedIn as well as Facebook in their leisure time. They read industry blogs and news features as well as trade magazines such as Hotel magazine.

01 Purpose
02 Intelligence
03 Proposition
04 Tools
05 Conversion
06 Results

2.2

Understanding your Customer: Customer Personas

ROLES & RESPONSIBILITIES (IF BUSINESS-TO-BUSINESS)		
What type of business do they operate in?		Hotel chain – could be business or leisure focused
What is their main role?		Sourcing and purchasing products
What are they responsible for?		All consumable products within hotel chain
Are they a key decision maker for your product / service?		Yes
What are their individual goals / objectives?		Showing savings for their company, sourcing products that complement the hotel's style, making a good impression on their own customers.

BUYING CYCLE		
How often do they buy your product / service? (Hourly, daily, weekly, monthly, annually or infrequent)		Order comes in monthly and will be renewed after 3/6/12 months.
What is their average spend? (per day / per week / per month / per year – choose which is the most applicable)		In the tens of thousands per month
Is price a decision factor for them when purchasing your product / service?		Yes due to purchasing large quantities
Where do they purchase? (online, telephone, instore or face-to-face)		Telephone, and they will have face to face meetings to secure the best deal
Are they loyal to you or do they shop around?		Shop around

01 Purpose
02 Intelligence
03 Proposition
04 Tools
05 Conversion
06 Results

2.3
Understanding your Competitors

Activity: Using customer motivations to make a sale

When considering your marketing, addressing the pain points you identified is crucial. In the box below, write the pain points you identified for each customer persona, and the solutions *your business* offers.

Your competitors probably have similar solutions to the same problems. How does your business go the extra mile?

2.3

Understanding your Customer: Customer Personas

CUSTOMER'S PAIN POINTS	YOUR SOLUTION	GO THE EXTRA MILE
Example: I work long hours and have little time to visit shops.	**Example:** Online shopping is available 24 hours a day, 7 days a week.	**Example:** Customer services are available by phone or web chat 24/7 to assist with queries and convert interest into sales. In the delivery box we include a voucher for 50% off their next purchase.

CUSTOMER'S PAIN POINTS	YOUR SOLUTION	GO THE EXTRA MILE

01 Purpose
02 Intelligence
03 Proposition
04 Tools
05 Conversion
06 Results

2.3
Understanding your Customer: Customer Personas

Great!

You now know there is a solid base of customers out there for your products or services.

You know who they are, what motivates them to purchase and the problems they experience. You've created solutions and you've gone the extra mile, **making sure you stand out.**

Be sure to use all of this intelligence in your marketing strategy – conveying these factors will be key to converting your target audience from interested parties to paying (and even loyal) customers.

01 Purpose
02 Intelligence
03 Proposition
04 Tools
05 Conversion
06 Results

2.3

Understanding your Customer: Customer Personas

Summary

You should now understand your customer (and consumer!). This includes:

Why it's important to define your target audience

How to create customer and consumer personas

How to focus your marketing on solving the pain points that your customers experience

01 Purpose
02 Intelligence
03 Proposition
04 Tools
05 Conversion
06 Results

2.3

Understanding your Customer: Customer Personas

Understanding your Competitors

Sometimes the intelligence we need is right in front of us: competitors can be an invaluable source of information and inspiration. Analysing them helps you set a firm basis for your marketing planning.

01 Purpose
02 Intelligence
03 Proposition
04 Tools
05 Conversion
06 Results

2.3

Understanding your Customer: Customer Personas

Why is a competitor analysis important?

Competitor analysis is about looking at which organisations pose a threat to you and how you operate within your market. Competitor analysis has many important roles in strategic planning, including:

To understand your business's advantages and disadvantages relative to competitors'.

To get a picture of the options available, from a customer's point of view.

To create a base for defining your organisation's USPs.

To understand and anticipate competitors' current and future marketing strategies.

To be fully informed before setting your marketing plan, increasing your chance of achieving competitive advantage.

01 Purpose
02 Intelligence
03 Proposition
04 Tools
05 Conversion
06 Results

2.3

Understanding your Customer: Customer Personas

Who are you competing with?

Initially it may seem obvious who your competitors are. But it's not always straightforward as so many factors affect customers' purchase decisions.

For example, Waitrose and Lidl are both supermarkets. Are they competitors?

No, they are not in direct competition.

Although they sell many of the same items, they have completely different target markets. One is luxury, the other budget. This affects the products they sell, the way they label goods, their marketing and even where their stores are located.

Think back to the pain points we discussed earlier. Thinking like one of your customers, what are their options? Say they work long hours, yes they could purchase from you – but who else offers the same solution?

Who offers more?

Your competitors may not be the same as you first thought.

01 Purpose
02 Intelligence
03 Proposition
04 Tools
05 Conversion
06 Results

2.3
Understanding your Customer: Customer Personas

Activity: Name your competitors

In the following box, write down the companies you consider your biggest competitors. Think about:

- *Who offers the same solutions to pain points?*

- *Are you thinking locally, nationally or worldwide?*

- *Who offers the same quality, the same features or the same price points?*

01 Purpose
02 Intelligence
03 Proposition
04 Tools
05 Conversion
06 Results

2.3

Understanding your Customer: Customer Personas

COMPETITORS

2.3
Understanding your Customer: Customer Personas

Activity: Your competitor analysis

Use this competitor analysis template to focus your thoughts on each of the competitors you identified. Ask yourself the questions you want answered to show how your competitors are doing, what they're doing and moreover, **you can learn from them.**

2.3
Understanding your Customer: Customer Personas

Competitor Analysis

GENERAL INFORMATION:	
Competitor name:	
Location:	
Years trading:	
Number of employees:	
Executive team and responsibilities:	
PRODUCTS / SERVICES:	
What do they sell?	
Where do they sell – local, regional or national?	
What makes their product / service attractive to their customers – what is their USP?	
What have they learned about their customer needs?	
What is their pricing strategy? Different tiers?	

01 Purpose
02 Intelligence
03 Proposition
04 Tools
05 Conversion
06 Results

2.3

Understanding your Customer: Customer Personas

MARKETING:	
Brand identity – modern or traditional?	
Website address:	
Google ranking – can they be found on the first two pages of Google?	
Keywords:	
Recent blog themes:	
Recent news:	
Social media networks:	
Social media activity – regular or irregular?	
Sales literature?	
Email activity – what messages are they pushing?	
Events – what kind of events do they attend?	
Any other media relevant to them?	
FINAL OBSERVATIONS:	
Risk to my business:	
Further comments / insight:	

2.3

Understanding your Customer: Customer Personas

Easy?

Did you find it easy to complete this table for each competitor?
If not, you may need to conduct further research into your competitors.
Great sources of information include:

- Market reports
- Competitors' websites
- Press releases
- Advertising campaigns
- Annual reports and accounts
- Trade shows
- Newspaper articles
- Promotions
- Conferences
- Price lists

- Social media
- Regulatory reports
- Customer conversations
- Trademark/Patent applications
- Your own network of contacts
- Customer surveys
- Trends and opinions
- Industry newsletters
- Desk research

01 Purpose
02 Intelligence
03 Proposition
04 Tools
05 Conversion
06 Results

2.3

Understanding your Customer: Customer Personas

Always keep monitoring your competitors.

Follow their social media efforts, regularly review their product range and sign up to their newsletters.

With this research, you can begin to articulate how your business provides a benefit to customers that your competitors can't or don't offer, and which is compelling enough to ***attract new customers.***

01 Purpose
02 Intelligence
03 Proposition
04 Tools
05 Conversion
06 Results

2.3
Understanding your Customer: Customer Personas

Checklist

You should now understand your competitors, including:

| ✓ | Why it's important to know what competitors are doing |

| ✓ | How to conduct a competitor analysis |

| ✓ | How competitors' activities will affect your own marketing plans |

01 Purpose
02 Intelligence
03 Proposition
04 Tools
05 Conversion
06 Results

2.4
Existing Data

Existing Data

You don't know what you don't know until you examine what you *do* know.

It makes perfect sense.

Existing data is a great source of intelligence.

It comes in many forms, from experience to facts and figures.

All is equally important and by combining it, we get a bigger picture of the industry.

New businesses may have little or no data, which is where knowledge and experience comes in useful.

01 Purpose
02 Intelligence
03 Proposition
04 Tools
05 Conversion
06 Results

2.4
Existing Data

Activity: The state of the current market

What do you currently know about the market you operate in? What intelligence do you have?
Let's start by considering what **you** have:

- A database of people interested in your products – such as from trade shows or a sign up on your website

- A database of previous customers

- Research you've carried out yourself, such as surveys

- Your own knowledge and experience of the industry

- Information on competitors and their activities

- Other:

01 Purpose
02 Intelligence
03 Proposition
04 Tools
05 Conversion
06 Results

2.4
Existing Data

What picture of the market does this give you?

CONSIDER WHAT YOU CAN EXTRAPOLATE FROM YOUR KNOWLEDGE...	
What are customers' attitudes?	
What do current and past trends show?	
Are more competitors popping up weekly?	

01 Purpose
02 Intelligence
03 Proposition
04 Tools
05 Conversion
06 Results

2.4

Existing Data

Next, we'll look at the third party (secondary) intelligence you have:

| Research on the industry, such as from marketing reports |

| Figures and statistics |

| Trends and forecasts |

| Other: |

01 Purpose
02 Intelligence
03 Proposition
04 Tools
05 Conversion
06 Results

2.4

Existing Data

What picture of the market does this give you?

CONSIDER THE STATE OF THE CURRENT MARKET...	
What does it look like?	
What does its future look like – is it set for growth?	
Think about positives and negatives, short term and long term.	

01 Purpose
02 Intelligence
03 Proposition
04 Tools
05 Conversion
06 Results

2.4
Existing Data

Where can you access more data?

If you are short on data, try looking into some of the sources identified earlier in the word cloud:

- Market reports
- Competitors' websites
- Press releases
- Advertising campaigns
- Annual reports and accounts
- Trade shows
- Newspaper articles
- Promotions
- Conferences
- Price lists
- Social media
- Regulatory reports
- Customer conversations
- Trademark/Patent applications
- Your own network of contacts
- Customer surveys
- Trends and opinions
- Industry newsletters
- Desk research

01 Purpose
02 Intelligence
03 Proposition
04 Tools
05 Conversion
06 Results

2.4

Existing Data

Activity: Let's play Snap

1.

Take your business values from the previous section and list them below in order of priority.

Next, consider your target customers' values, and list those in order of priority.

How much do they differ?

MY BUSINESS VALUES	MY CUSTOMERS BUSINESS VALUES

01 Purpose
02 Intelligence
03 Proposition
04 Tools
05 Conversion
06 Results

2.4
Existing Data

2.

Now, consider one of your competitors. List the values they communicate in the third column.

Whose values best match the target customers'?
Hopefully the answer is yours.

If not, it may be time to reconsider your values in terms of what is really important to your customers.

YOUR BRAND VALUES (IN ORDER OF PRIORITY)	YOUR TARGET CUSTOMERS' VALUES (IN ORDER OF PRIORITY)	A COMPETITORS' VALUES (IN ORDER OF PRIORITY)
1.		
2.		
3.		
4.		
5.		

01 Purpose
02 Intelligence
03 Proposition
04 Tools
05 Conversion
06 Results

2.4

Existing Data

Summary

You should now understand how to gain intelligence from your existing data. ***This includes:***

1 What types of data you hold and where to find more

2 How to take an objective, 360 degree view of the market to forecast future trends

3 What factors will affect sales in your industry

01 Purpose
02 Intelligence
03 Proposition
04 Tools
05 Conversion
06 Results

2.5
Understanding your SWOT

And finally... Understanding your SWOT

(Strengths, Weaknesses, Opportunities and Threats)

Before embarking on any marketing activity, it's essential to understand the environment your business currently operates in.

This form of business intelligence will enable you to make more informed decisions, based on threats and opportunities associated with your area of business.

01 Purpose
02 Intelligence
03 Proposition
04 Tools
05 Conversion
06 Results

2.5
Understanding your SWOT

We begin by performing a SWOT analysis on your current business.

SWOT analysis (Strengths/Weaknesses/Opportunities/Threats)

The SWOT analysis model was invented in the 1960s by a management consultant named Albert Humphrey at the Stanford Research Institute. Conducting a SWOT analysis will help you analyse your business, identifying areas that may need attention as well as realising opportunities that may not have been considered previously.

A **S**trength is a positive internal factor such as your specialist expertise, innovative product or high quality service.

A **W**eakness is also an internal factor such as lack of knowledge or expertise, location of your business or poor brand image.

An **O**pportunity is a positive external factor such as a new developing market where you have experience, or where competition is weak and unstable.

A **T**hreat is a negative external factor such as a new competitor operating in your market, aggressive pricing wars, launch of a new innovate product or service which supersedes your own.

2.5
Understanding your SWOT

A SWOT analysis will provide an honest and objective view of your business, enabling you to determine where you are now and where you want your business to be in the future.

You can utilise your knowledge and understanding of your existing customers and competitors to record more accurate analysis.

01	Purpose
02	Intelligence
03	Proposition
04	Tools
05	Conversion
06	Results

2.5

Understanding your SWOT

POSITIVE FACTORS

STRENGTHS
Describes what a business excels at and what separates it from the competition. These are the 'internal' positive attributes, tangible and intangible, to your business.

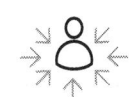

OPPORTUNITIES
The 'external' positive factors that represent reasons for your business to grow and prosper. Consider customer 'pain points' – obstacles, issues or problems they encounter which you can provide a solution for.

INTERNAL FACTORS

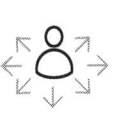

EXTERNAL FACTORS

SWOT ANALYSIS

WEAKNESSES
The areas within your business, which may affect the value you offer, or place you in a competitive disadvantage. These are the areas you can enhance in order to compete with your best competitor.

THREATS
These are the external factors beyond your control that could place your strategy, or the business itself, at risk. Example – a competitor who has access to greater resources than you such as finance or technology.

NEGITIVE FACTORS

01 Purpose
02 Intelligence
03 Proposition
04 Tools
05 Conversion
06 Results

2.5
Understanding your SWOT

Activity: Your SWOT analysis

Based on the SWOT Analysis model on the previous page, use the template following to list your business's internal strengths and weaknesses, as well as the external opportunities and threats it faces in the marketplace.

01 Purpose
02 Intelligence
03 Proposition
04 Tools
05 Conversion
06 Results

2.5

Understanding your SWOT

SWOT ANALYSIS	
STRENGTHS	**WEAKNESSES**
Describes what your business excels at and what separates it from the competition. These are the 'internal' positive attributes, tangible and intangible, to your business.	The areas within your business, which may affect the value you offer, or place you in a competitive disadvantage. These are the areas you can enhance in order to compete with your best competitor.

01 Purpose
02 Intelligence
03 Proposition
04 Tools
05 Conversion
06 Results

2.5

Understanding your SWOT

SWOT ANALYSIS	
OPPORTUNITIES	**THREATS**
The 'external' positive factors that represent reasons for your business to grow and prosper. Consider customer 'pain points' – obstacles, issues or problems they encounter which you can provide a solution for.	These are the external factors beyond your control that could place your strategy, or the business itself, at risk. Example – a competitor who has access to greater resources than you such as finance or technology.

2.5

Understanding your SWOT

Using Analysis Tools

After completing this analysis you should now have a bigger picture of your business in the context of the market it operates in.

The SWOT tool helps you remain objective and may have uncovered opportunities you haven't previously considered, or shown strengths you can utilise in your marketing strategy.

The tools prepare you for external events that you have no control over and that may impact your business – such as new legislation coming into force.
Many large organisations have gone out of business because their external market changed and they failed to plan and keep up with the market.

Remember Blockbuster and LoveFilm, the postal DVD rental service? They were both extremely popular businesses that failed to plan and keep up with the ever-changing environment.

Despite their many benefits, tools such as SWOT do have their limitations. They must not be used in isolation – they serve as a guide but further information and planning is needed to determine the best solutions.

01 Purpose
02 Intelligence
03 Proposition
04 Tools
05 Conversion
06 Results

2.5

Understanding your SWOT

Top tip

To make the most of SWOT, make sure your statements are based on facts (and statistics where possible), and not assumptions.

2.5
Understanding your SWOT

Summary

You should now understand how to carry out a SWOT analysis, including:

1	Why it's important to analyse the market you operate in.

2	How to use look at the market in depth and objectively

3	The benefits and limitations of tools such as SWOT

01 Purpose
02 Intelligence
03 Proposition
04 Tools
05 Conversion
06 Results

2.6
Summary and implementing these principles

Section summary and implementing these principles

Throughout this section we have looked at business intelligence in several forms.

We've explored the types of intelligence that is available, how to gather more and how to analyse the market.

Examining this intelligence allows us to make informed decisions in the context of the market as a whole. It helps us take into account both internal and external factors, and plan for risk before it occurs.

We have examined target audience in detail, creating customer personas and identifying their pain points in order to find solutions – which we can then promote through marketing activity.

Knowing what competitors are doing and how exactly your business differs from them means we are in the advantageous position of knowing what we can offer customers and how we can stand out. This will feed into the USPs we will look at in the next section.

If you've used tools like SWOT previously, you may find your answers have changed as your business has become more established. This is a positive – it shows growth and experience. External factors will always affect how your business operates, and continuing to carry out analysis periodically will give you further depth of insight.

01 Purpose
02 Intelligence
03 Proposition
04 Tools
05 Conversion
06 Results

2.6
Summary and implementing these principles

Implementing these Principles

By spending time gathering and analysing this intelligence, we are much better placed to make focused, informed decisions and to mitigate risk. We avoid becoming blinkered by our own experience and can instead focus on facts and trends to produce reliable forecasts.

01 Purpose
02 Intelligence
03 Proposition
04 Tools
05 Conversion
06 Results

2.6
Summary and implementing these principles

Taking your learning forward

• *Clearly communicate* your customer and consumer personas to your employees at all levels – if they understand who they are dealing with, they can offer a better service and respond to their needs more effectively.

• *Continue to carry out research regularly* – the environment you operate in is constantly changing, as are customer needs and preferences. Stay ahead of the game and plan ahead.

• *Bad feedback* is as valuable as good feedback – if you can find out why people don't buy from you, they may give simple solutions that open the door to more sales.

• *Be open* to what market trends show – sometimes all the planning in the world can't predict how customers behave. Who would have predicted we'd need text messaging 30 years ago? Look at the figures, listen to feedback and act on it.

• *There's a reason* that large organisations invest in research and development. If you're not sure you're solving the right problems for your target audience, ask them. Focus groups, surveys and test products can be very valuable.

01 Purpose
02 Intelligence
03 Proposition
04 Tools
05 Conversion
06 Results

2.6
Summary and implementing these principles

Checklist

The checklist below provides a plan and further points to consider that will consolidate the learning in this section.

- I have carried out a SWOT analysis to understand the internal and external factors that affect my business.
- I know my customers and consumers, and what pain points my products/services solve for them.
- I have examined my competitors and understand what factors we are competing on and why customers may choose to use them.
- I am confident I have a good range of data on which I can base decisions.
- I understand how customers and consumers respond to marketing messages that solve their pain points.

01 Purpose
02 Intelligence
03 Proposition
04 Tools
05 Conversion
06 Results

03

Proposition

01 Purpose
02 Intelligence
03 Proposition
04 Tools
05 Conversion
06 Results

03
Proposition

"Strategy is based on a differentiated customer value proposition. Satisfying customers is the source of sustainable value creation."

Kaplan and Norton, 2004

03
Proposition

Proposition

Most of us have been propositioned
once or twice in our life.
But did you realise that businesses proposition us all the time? They have a Unique Selling Proposition (USP) – a promise of value to be delivered, communicated and acknowledged. The proposition sets the belief of a customer about how value will be delivered and experienced.

In this section we'll look at:

1 **Why** is a USP important?

2 **How** do you get your USP spot on?

3 **What** are positioning statements and why do I need them?

4 **How** does all of this feed into key messages?

www.marketingskillsacademy.co.uk

01 Purpose
02 Intelligence
03 Proposition
04 Tools
05 Conversion
06 Results

03
Proposition

Your 'Proposition' Model

Your Unique Selling Proposition (USP) — What sets you apart from your competitors

+

Your Positioning Statement — Will help you communicate and deliver your USP to your target market

+

Your Key Messages — Bite-size phrases that communicate what you do, what you stand for and how you are different

=

PROPOSITION

01 Purpose
02 Intelligence
03 Proposition
04 Tools
05 Conversion
06 Results

3.1
Why is a Unique Selling Proposition (USP) important?

Why is a Unique Selling Proposition (USP) important?

Your business is NOT selling a product or service.

It is **NOT** selling time or an experience.

It **IS** selling an **'outcome'** – a perception of value, which your customer has already desired and is open to receive. This may be a product or service, which requires a change of mindset, a new life experience, working practice or general wellbeing from one situation to another.

Therefore, to be successful in business, you need to have a

Unique Selling Proposition

- or USP for short.

01 Purpose
02 Intelligence
03 Proposition
04 Tools
05 Conversion
06 Results

3.1
Why is a Unique Selling Proposition (USP) important?

Your USP and Differentiation

Your unique selling proposition should be what sets you apart from the competition. Just as the name suggests, a "unique" selling proposition must explain what distinguishes your business or offering. You may have a product or service which is new to the market, or it may be the way in which you present it to your customers.

Either way, it is essential that you define the particular advantages your company has **over the competition**.

When you consider your USP, think about the ways in which you solve your target markets' 'pain points' like no other.

However, you need to be specific as generic-sounding claims about customer service or simply being 'the best' are not always effective.

3.1
Why is a Unique Selling Proposition (USP) important?

How do you communicate your value proposition in your marketing?

Simply by following these steps:

1. First, your marketing needs to understand what 'value perception' you are offering – what is your unique selling proposition (USP), which differentiates you from your competitors.
Types of 'differentiation' include:

• **Product differentiation** – your product offers better features, functionality, performance, style or design

• **Service differentiation** – you offer extra service, such as fast delivery, longer opening hours or better customer care

• **Channel differentiation** – differentiating your channel's coverage (i.e. how you market and deliver your product or service), expertise and performance

• **People differentiation** – hiring and training better people than competitors do, to offer a better purchase experience – post, during and after purchase

• **Image differentiation** – your brand is a status symbol, e.g. BMW or Audi

01 Purpose
02 Intelligence
03 Proposition
04 Tools
05 Conversion
06 Results

3.1
Why is a Unique Selling Proposition (USP) important?

2.

Next, align your value proposition to the types of 'ideal customer' – based on your customer personas (which we covered in Section 2), who desire to gain that value through your product or service. Here we develop your positioning statement.

3.

Finally, structure your proposition using key messages in order to engage and communicate with your ideal customer and convert them into a sale.

4.

Once we have achieved this, you then look to deliver the value proposition using the most effective and appropriate marketing channels and activities – which we'll go into in the next section.

3.1
Why is a Unique Selling Proposition (USP) important?

Summary

You should now understand why defining your USP is important. This includes:

1	*The value customers are looking for*

2	*The types of differentiation*

3	*How to communicate your value proposition in your marketing*

3.2
Why is a Unique Selling Proposition (USP) important?

How do you define your own USP?

Effective USPs identify the most important benefits of using your services, solve an industry pain point, and (of course) are unique. Once you've determined yours, this can be integrated into all your marketing collateral and customer communication tools – more on that later.

01 Purpose
02 Intelligence
03 Proposition
04 Tools
05 Conversion
06 Results

3.2
Why is a Unique Selling Proposition (USP) important?

Virgin

'Holiday like a Rockstar'

In 2011 Virgin Holidays launched a campaign inviting customers to 'Holiday like a Rockstar'.

Virgin Holidays' marketing manager said, "The long-haul market is not growing at the moment, so it is critical that we shout very loudly as a business about what we stand for, which is what the Rockstar Service campaign is all about."

As part of the campaign, marketing focused on the experiences customers could have on holiday – it showed how Virgin Holidays' service made them feel special. It pictured couples and families having the time of their lives and experiencing adventures they never before imagined.

The company addressed a market condition – the long haul market not growing. They knew their customer personas well and their solution – the value they offered – was to make holidays something new, something exciting. Giving them more than they bargained for. The line 'Holiday like a Rockstar' alone allows the customer to conjure up their own images of what they can expect. The marketing developed from this plays on feelings and experiences, which creates the company's promise of value to be delivered.

01 Purpose
02 Intelligence
03 Proposition
04 Tools
05 Conversion
06 Results

3.2
Why is a Unique Selling Proposition (USP) important?

The Real Question

So the real question is, what do your target market want that your competitors aren't offering them? (Or perhaps competitors are offering this but the price/place/other variable isn't right – it doesn't suit the customer persona.)

3.2
Why is a Unique Selling Proposition (USP) important?

Activity: Solving problems to create your USP

You know your customer personas – what are the principal pain points your target customers have which you could solve with your value proposition?

Tip: Keep it focused – you're trying to solve the biggest problems for your identified target market. Concentrate on one or two major problems you can solve.

1.

2.

3.2
Why is a Unique Selling Proposition (USP) important?

Now, what benefits does your company offer that solves these pain points?

1. _____
2. _____
3. _____
4. _____

Finally, reword your benefits so they are addressing the pain points you identified. Keep it short – USPs are not introductory paragraphs. They are generally a phrase or sentence. Don't ramble. The more concise you are, the better your results will be.

01 Purpose
02 Intelligence
03 Proposition
04 Tools
05 Conversion
06 Results

3.2
Why is a Unique Selling Proposition (USP) important?

Examples:

Domino's Pizza:
You get fresh, hot pizza delivered to your door in 30 minutes or less or it's free.

FedEx Corporation:
When it absolutely, positively has to be there overnight.

Avis:
We're number two. We try harder.

Congratulations - you've just written your unique selling proposition!

01 Purpose
02 Intelligence
03 Proposition
04 Tools
05 Conversion
06 Results

3.2
Why is a Unique Selling Proposition (USP) important?

Summary

You should now have written your USP. You should also understand:

1 *The benefits of what you offer*

2 *Why your marketing needs to solve problems for your customers*

3 *How to communicate your ability to solve these problems*

What are Positioning Statements and why do I need them?

Positioning Statements help you communicate and deliver your USP to the target market. Stood alone, it may not be evident who your USP is aimed at. Positioning Statements align your USP to your ideal target customer, based on the customer personas you have written.

3.3
What are Positioning Statements and why do I need them?

Here's our 3 awesome tips to create effective Positioning Statements:

1. *Identify* a set of possible competitive advantages to build a position i.e. why are you better than the competition?

2. *Choose* the right competitive advantages – keep going back to your customer personas. What do they care about? What are their pain points? What features are or aren't important to them?

3. *Select* an overall positioning strategy – where can you deliver superior value for your customer? As outlined earlier, this could be from:

> Product differentiation <
> Services differentiation <
> Channel differentiation <
> People differentiation <
> Image differentiation <

01 Purpose
02 Intelligence
03 Proposition
04 Tools
05 Conversion
06 Results

3.3
What are Positioning Statements and why do I need them?

Here's a really simple way to break down a Positioning Statement to summarise your company or brand positioning:

For **(customer persona and need)**,
(business / brand)
offers **(concept)**
because **(point of difference)**.

———————— *For example…* ————————

For **young professional people seeking stress-busting relaxation services**,
The Health & Beauty Club
offers **natural health, relaxation and beauty services and retreats**
because **we have an unrivalled reputation for delivering high quality wellness services in our state-of-the-art club**

3.3

What are Positioning Statements and why do I need them?

Activity: Create a positioning statement

Use the above model to create a positioning statement for your brand.

For **(customer persona and need)**, **(business / brand)** offers **(concept)** because **(point of difference)**.

---

01 Purpose
02 Intelligence
03 Proposition
04 Tools
05 Conversion
06 Results

3.3
What are Positioning Statements and why do I need them?

Summary

You should now understand what positioning statements are and why you need them, including:

1 *Using your competitive advantage*

2 *How to write effective positioning statements*

3.4
How does all of this feed into key messages?

How does all of this feed into key messages?

Key sales messages are basically bite-sized phrases or summations, based on your USP, that communicate: what you do, what you stand for and how you are different to other businesses. They will form the foundations for all future marketing activity, providing clear and consistent brand messages.

> Think of your key messages as ways of communicating the benefits you offer – you have thousands of potential customers, and they all want to know – 'what's in it for me?' – this is your chance to tell them!

Your messages are very visible to customers, to competitors and to the world – time to show off what you can really offer!

01 Purpose
02 Intelligence
03 Proposition
04 Tools
05 Conversion
06 Results

3.4
How does all of this feed into key messages?

Let's look at some other key messages and the problem they are addressing:

BRAND	KEY MESSAGE	WHY DOES IT APPEAL TO CUSTOMERS what's it telling them?
Uber	Tap the app. Get a ride	Simplicity
Apple	There's nothing quite like iPhone	Image differentiation
Mercedes-Benz	Engineered to move the human spirit	Emotional, brand differentiation

3.4
How does all of this feed into key messages?

Top tip: Think about your industry and positioning strategy when developing your key messages:

A company selling food products may focus their key messages on tastes, flavours, scents and sights. Business to business companies may focus on more tangible benefits, such as cost savings, faster turnaround timescales or the introduction of new technologies.

01 Purpose
02 Intelligence
03 Proposition
04 Tools
05 Conversion
06 Results

3.4
How does all of this feed into key messages?

Brand language

When writing key messages or any text aimed at the consumer, consider your 'brand language' – the distinct words you use to reflect your brand's 'personality'.

It is also affected by the method of differentiation you choose. For example, a company selling artisan cheese and differentiating on product (*'this is the best cheese available'*) may concentrate its brand language around:

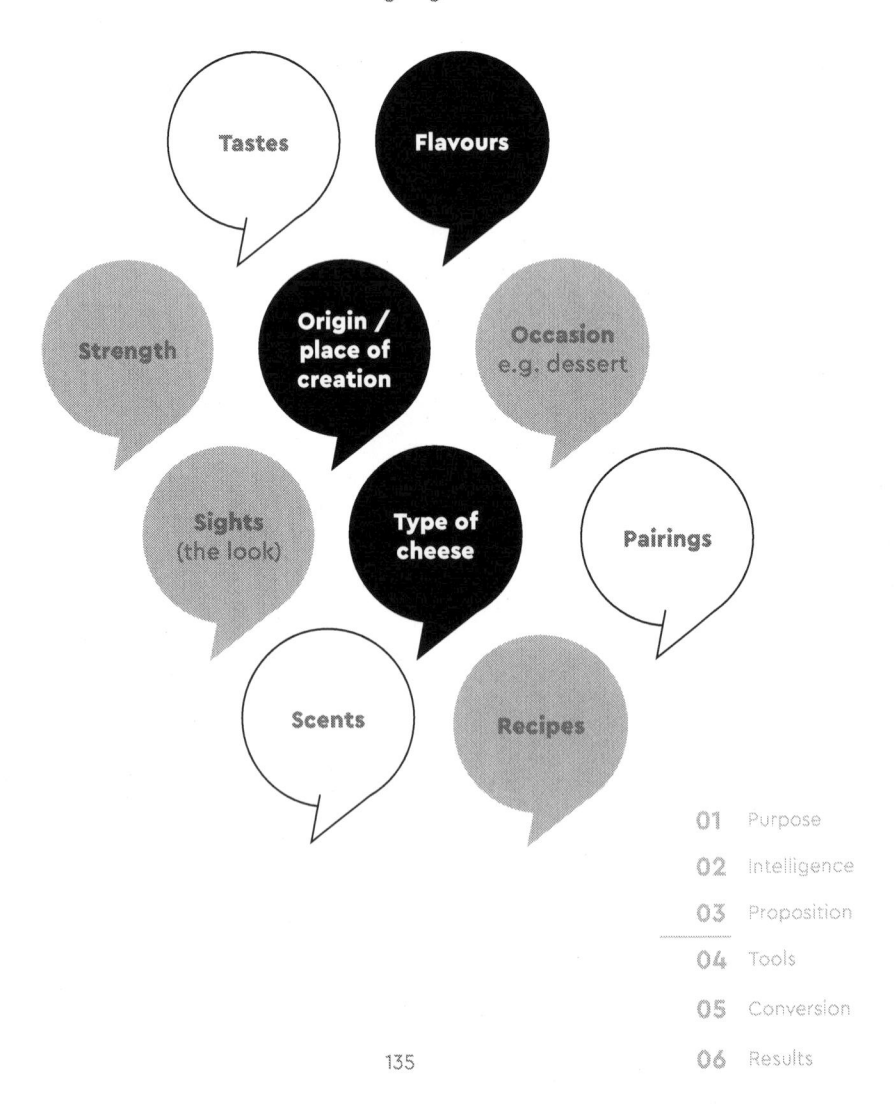

- Tastes
- Flavours
- Strength
- Origin / place of creation
- Occasion e.g. dessert
- Sights (the look)
- Type of cheese
- Pairings
- Scents
- Recipes

01 Purpose
02 Intelligence
03 Proposition
04 Tools
05 Conversion
06 Results

3.4
How does all of this feed into key messages?

Focus

By focusing its brand language on the senses, the cheese company makes it easy for the reader to **visualise themselves buying and enjoying the product.**

The company wants people to read their language and conjure up images, make their mouth water and give them ideas they can't wait to try.

3.4

How does all of this feed into key messages?

TOP TIP:

Always try and keep your key messages:

Jargon-free
especially when using any technical terms or explanations

Consistent
across all marketing channels

On point
don't complicate matters or confuse your audience with lots of words or over explaining

01 Purpose
02 Intelligence
03 Proposition
04 Tools
05 Conversion
06 Results

3.4
How does all of this feed into key messages?

Activity: Craft your key messages

ASK YOURSELF, WHAT DO YOU WANT THE TARGET AUDIENCES TO HEAR AND REMEMBER?

3.4
How does all of this feed into key messages?

Checklist for your key messages – are they:

- [ ] Conversational
- [ ] Concise
- [ ] Aligned with your USP
- [ ] The same tone as your brand – if your brand is fun but your key messages are formal, they won't ring true with customers
- [ ] Tailored to your customer personas
- [ ] Meaningful
- [ ] Engaging
- [ ] Simple
- [ ] Memorable

3.4

How does all of this feed into key messages?

Summary

You should now understand what key messages are and why you need them, including:

1	Communicating the benefits of your offer
2	Using the right brand language
3	How to write effective key messages

01 Purpose
02 Intelligence
03 Proposition
04 Tools
05 Conversion
06 Results

04

Tools

04
Tools

"There's a simple rule: You say it again, and you say it again, and you say it again, and you say it again, and you say it again, and then again and again and again and again, and about the time that you're absolutely sick of saying it is about the time that your target audience has heard it for the first time."

Frank Luntz, political consultant, public opinion guru

01 Purpose
02 Intelligence
03 Proposition
04 Tools
05 Conversion
06 Results

04
Tools

Tools

This section is your guide to the marketing tools available and how they should be used. It's designed as a hands-on resource that you can refer back to at any point.

In this section we'll look at:

1	***The marketing tools available:*** the good, the bad and the ugly
2	***How*** to choose the right tools
3	***Types of campaign***, route to market and other variables

01 Purpose
02 Intelligence
03 Proposition
04 Tools
05 Conversion
06 Results

04
Tools

Your 'Tools' Model

- Selection
- Evaluation Adv vs Dis
- Intentions
= TOOLS

01 Purpose
02 Intelligence
03 Proposition
04 Tools
05 Conversion
06 Results

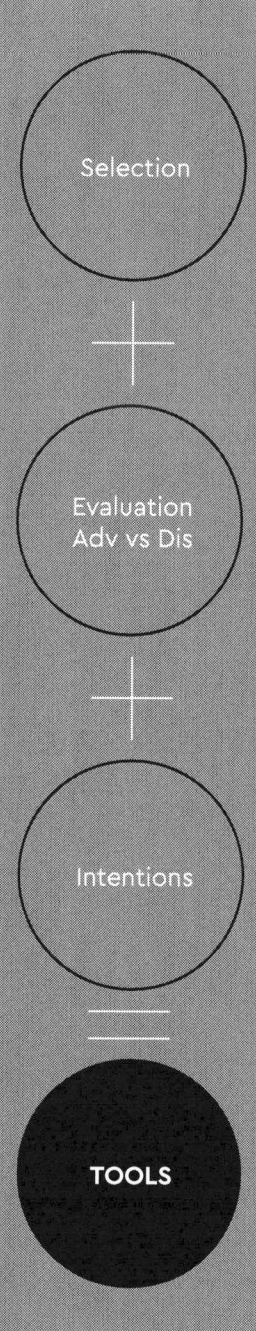

4.0
Tools

Marketing Tools

It's surprising how many businesses still use lots of different marketing tools – often at great expense – and still don't know the effectiveness of each one. Many wouldn't know where they get a return on investment and where money is going down the drain.

[*The key to effective marketing campaigns is recognising that not all things work for all people, and the things that do work don't work without a solid plan behind them.*]

So while marketing isn't an exact science and never will be, strategy plays a huge role. Carefully selecting the tools we use to communicate with and engage audiences means that waste is kept to a minimum, and conversion rates are pushed to their maximum.

01 Purpose
02 Intelligence
03 Proposition
04 Tools
05 Conversion
06 Results

4.0

Tools

How to choose your tools

The tools you choose are also known as your tactics – your way of attracting customers.

The key with choosing your tools is to refer back to your customer personas. These should have given you insight into who you're communicating with, and where/how they'll receive your messages. Of course, there are other factors that will affect your choice, including:

1	Budget
2	Timeframe
3	Industry
4	What competitors are doing

01 Purpose
02 Intelligence
03 Proposition
04 Tools
05 Conversion
06 Results

4.0
Tools

It is however essential that you:

✓ **Use a combination of tools** – everyone consumes media and remembers in different ways. Don't rely on one tool. Using different media increases the likelihood of someone remembering your message. Remember the customer journey from section 1 – think about how many touchpoints you want the average person in your target market to receive. Not everyone will see all communications you put out.

✓ **Repetition, repetition, repetition** – the more your customer hears something, the more likely they are to remember it. And when they have a need for your product or service, your brand will be at the forefront of their memory.

Repetition also build **credibility** – if someone remembers your brand, they are unconsciously biased toward it. This comes into play every day with brand names in supermarkets. They consistently sell in higher volumes than own brand products – because customers are familiar with them, and because they like the brand, there is a high perceived value.

01 Purpose
02 Intelligence
03 Proposition
04 Tools
05 Conversion
06 Results

4.0
Tools

Drip vs burst campaigns

Your marketing may fall into the category of either a drip or burst campaign.

With a drip campaign, activity is spread out over a long time period so the customer continually hears about what you have to offer. As an example, we're probably all aware of a sofa retailer who seems to always be holding a sale.
Drip campaigns can be a great strategy as messages are reinforced at various points in time, meaning your brand is never far from the target markets' minds.

A burst campaign is where you focus a large campaign on a short space of time, maximising the channels and frequency of messages so your customers hear them again and again. Burst campaigns are great for new product launches, seasonal items and any product or service that is trend or time specific. A good example would be when a new film is released – you may see it promoted on billboards, in TV ads, with actors doing interviews – and then a month later the messages have vanished. The high frequency of messages builds excitement and makes the product more memorable.

Will your marketing be short term or long term – drip or burst?

01 Purpose
02 Intelligence
03 Proposition
04 Tools
05 Conversion
06 Results

4.0 Tools

Top tip: Route to market

If you're selling products, consider your route to market – the way your customers purchase your product.

This will affect the tactics you use. Some routes to market are:

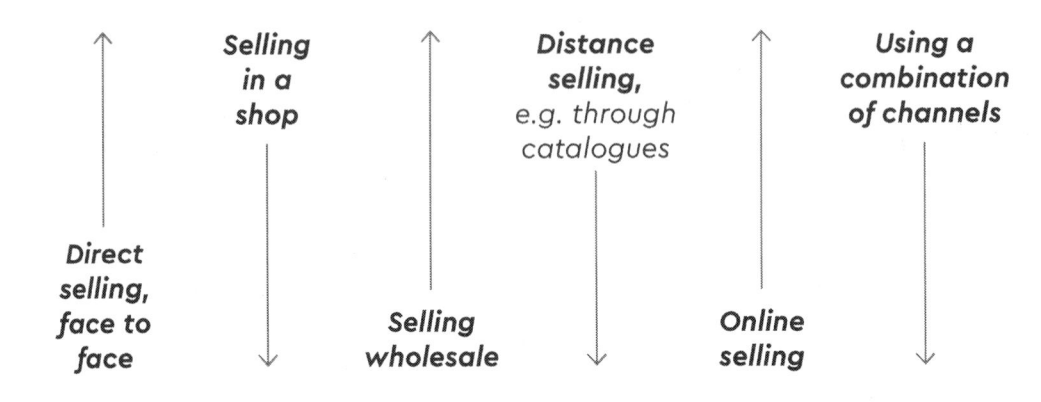

- *Direct selling, face to face*
- *Selling in a shop*
- *Selling wholesale*
- *Distance selling, e.g. through catalogues*
- *Online selling*
- *Using a combination of channels*

4.0

Tools

Brand identity

Your brand identity, or branding, is the perceived image and subsequent emotional response to a company, its products and services. It allows you to engage with customers and distinguish your company from competitors.

01 Purpose
02 Intelligence
03 Proposition
04 Tools
05 Conversion
06 Results

4.0
Tools

IN YOUR TOOLKIT				
	Advantages	**Disadvantages**	**When to use**	**When not to use**
Logo and brand consistency	Present your identity to consumers and customers; reinforce who you are; identify yourself in new places to raise awareness	Must be consistent or this can cause problems with the messages customers receive	Always for any company engaging with any audience	Only not relevant for holding companies and similar that never have contact with any audiences
Brand personality and tone of voice	Present your identity to consumers and customers; show what you stand for; create engagement and interest	None as long as you are authentic and consistent	In all communication with customers, formal and informal	Internally (though some companies prefer to continue their ethos internally)

01 Purpose
02 Intelligence
03 Proposition
04 Tools
05 Conversion
06 Results

4.0

Tools

	Advantages	Disadvantages	When to use	When not to use
	IN YOUR TOOLKIT			
Workwear	Presents a united front; identifies your workers; protective equipment (PPE) is often necessary	Costly; workers may act unfavourably while in uniform outside work	Where PPE is needed; when you want to provide reassurance; when customers are face to face with staff on site (your premises or theirs)	When not required for safety and customers will never see staff face to face
Promotional merchandise	Get your name in front of audiences with branded items they use	Difficult to track results; often gives a low return on investment; raises awareness but nothing more	When you need to remind customers who you are; when there is a significant time between purchases, e.g. insurance companies selling annual policies	When other avenues would prove more cost effective

01 Purpose
02 Intelligence
03 Proposition
04 Tools
05 Conversion
06 Results

4.0
Tools

Digital Marketing

This includes any activity that consumers can see online – including on their mobiles.

IN YOUR TOOLKIT				
	Advantages	Disadvantages	When to use	When not to use
Your website	Huge opportunities; your digital storefront; you have full control	Needs to be updated regularly	24/7. It is the 'hub' of all your marketing and should sit at the centre of all activity	When you're 100% sure your customer, consumer and influencers won't be online
Search engine optimisation (SEO)	Better ranking on search engines; increased website traffic; more targeted website traffic	Costly; requires specialist knowledge or external agency; lots of competition; requires constant attention; takes many months to see results	When you have a website and you need to drive more targeted traffic to it; when you have a lot of competitors offering similar products/services; to take customers from awareness to engagement and purchase	Low involvement purchase decision; where cost would be better spent elsewhere; when your website is not an important touchpoint

01 Purpose
02 Intelligence
03 Proposition
04 Tools
05 Conversion
06 Results

4.0

Tools

	Advantages	Disadvantages	When to use	When not to use
Online advertising	Targeted; trackable	Can be costly; messages must be very concise; many people have ad blockers	As part of a larger campaign	As the first (or only) touchpoint on the customer journey
Pay per click (PPC) advertising	Very targeted way of advertising; trackable; easy to control budgets	Can be costly; messages must be very concise	On specific websites/social media relevant to your customer personas	As the first (or only) touchpoint on the customer journey
Forums	Ability to engage with customers and their opinion	Not measurable; lot of time required	When opinions and word of mouth is important	When resource could be better spent elsewhere

4.0

Tools

IN YOUR TOOLKIT				
	Advantages	**Disadvantages**	**When to use**	**When not to use**
Social media	Huge reach; full control over your messages; free	A large following requires continual effort	For all customer facing companies, and many business to business ones too	When you're confident few to none of your customers are on social media themselves
Email marketing	Targeted; low cost; engaged audience	Can be seen as spammy if content and frequency isn't right	For regular updates and launches; news of interest to the customer	Too often or when you have nothing of interest to say
Website analytics	See how many visitors you have; what performs well; track conversions	Difficult to tell **why** people don't convert	If you have a website	If you don't have a website

01 Purpose
02 Intelligence
03 Proposition
04 Tools
05 Conversion
06 Results

4.0
Tools

Content Marketing

		Advantages	Disadvantages	When to use	When not to use
		\multicolumn{4}{c	}{**IN YOUR TOOLKIT**}
Blogs		Complete control over content; gain a captive audience and regular following; low cost; opportunity to respond to market changes and trends	Can be difficult to get content right to provide real value to your audience	When relevant to your company or products; fast changing markets affected by trends	When it doesn't fit your customer personas
Influencers, bloggers and vloggers		Excellent for trends such as consumables and fashion	Often high cost for little gain	When word of mouth is important	If it doesn't fit your customer personas
Videos		Complete control over content; clips can be shared on social media; allows for sign ups	Can be difficult to drive traffic; can be high cost and time consuming to create	When visuals help 'sell' your product or service, when you have a lot of information to impart	When it doesn't fit your customer personas; when time and cost would be better spent elsewhere

01 Purpose
02 Intelligence
03 Proposition
04 Tools
05 Conversion
06 Results

4.0
Tools

	Advantages	Disadvantages	When to use	When not to use
White papers	Complete control over content; position your company as an industry authority; introduce new ideas	Little room for engagement; no immediate follow up; may not get picked up by other news agencies	Developing industries; for new products and ideas; newsworthy information or developments; introducing new approaches or ways of thinking	Low involvement purchase decisions; when customers would get no value from them
Infographics	Super-powerful marketing tool that makes complex information and data easy to understand	Can be over-complicated if too much data or poor graphic execution	When educating your audience regarding "heavy" topics in an enjoyable way. Visuals help readers process the content more efficiently.	When it doesn't fit your customer personas; when time and cost would be better spent elsewhere

4.0

Tools

	Advantages	Disadvantages	When to use	When not to use
IN YOUR TOOLKIT				
Podcasts	They offer a personal connection with your audience as well as promote your expertise level; they provide a repeat 'touch-point' as most are repeatedly listened too whilst on the move	They need time to plan, script and create as well as knowledge of technology required.	If you're camera shy and video isn't an option, Podcasts are great for growing your audience as well as reaching out to new audiences and build familiarity with your brand.	If you or your audience is time-poor; low involvement purchase decisions; if you're not a confident speaker
Webinars	Complete control over content; two way engagement; allows sharing of ideas; opportunity to create excitement and interest	Can be difficult to encourage sign ups; must be held at a time convenient to target audience	Specialist subjects where more information may be needed to encourage purchase	Low involvement purchase decisions; when target customer is time poor

01 Purpose
02 Intelligence
03 Proposition
04 Tools
05 Conversion
06 Results

4.0
Tools

Print collateral

This includes any printed materials – their popularity has died down since the introduction of the internet, but used carefully they can be very powerful.

	IN YOUR TOOLKIT			
	Advantages	Disadvantages	When to use	When not to use
Sales literature: brochures, posters, flyers, leaflets	Prime way to print information on your brand and demonstrate your USP	Can be costly; many customers will only glance at it or ignore it completely	When it fits with other marketing – e.g. brochures to take to meetings and trade shows	For overly detailed information – this can be given at the enquiry/sale stage
Packaging	Free rein to convey your brand message	Space is often limited	When the end customer will see the packaging	If it will be costly and packaging is disposed of immediately

01 Purpose
02 Intelligence
03 Proposition
04 Tools
05 Conversion
06 Results

4.0

Tools

IN YOUR TOOLKIT

	Advantages	Disadvantages	When to use	When not to use
Coupons	Incentive to purchase quickly	Use too often and customers may not buy at full price	To encourage people to trial your product or service	For high end or luxury goods/services – this could devalue the perceived worth
Print advertising	Can be targeted; lots of space for branding and messaging	Market is flooded and content can be ignored; can be costly depending on placement	In targeted publications relevant to your target market	When not targeted
On building and external branding, including vehicle livery	Eye catching	Can be expensive	To increase visibility of your brand identity	When your target market aren't geographically near your building or vehicles

01 Purpose
02 Intelligence
03 Proposition
04 Tools
05 Conversion
06 Results

4.0
Tools

	Advantages	Disadvantages	When to use	When not to use
IN YOUR TOOLKIT			
Pull up banners/ display systems	Great for portraying your brand, especially at trade shows and events	Used by many in events and may not stand out or be memorable	Trade shows; events; conferences; your premises; point of sale where appropriate	When you have a lot of info to convey
Point of sale display (POS)	Eye catching; memorable; can build brand loyalty	High initial cost	When the customer or consumer will view it	POS can be difficult to implement due to retailers' own rules

4.0
Tools

Public Relations (PR)

PR is the practice of managing the spread of information between an individual or an organisation and the public. The activity is usually free (though you may pay an agency to look after it for you).

IN YOUR TOOLKIT

	Advantages	Disadvantages	When to use	When not to use
Press releases	Great way to spread messages; press coverage is highly influencing	May not be picked up by press; no control over how it will be edited	Company announcements; when there is interesting news; new product launches new markets entered	When there is no 'valuable' information to share
Events and trade shows	Meet people with a genuine interest in your products/services; targeted audience; face to face contact; networking	Lots of competition; difficult to engage many people at once	When relevant events arrive	When attendees aren't your target customers or consumers

01 Purpose
02 Intelligence
03 Proposition
04 Tools
05 Conversion
06 Results

4.0

Tools

IN YOUR TOOLKIT

	Advantages	Disadvantages	When to use	When not to use
Speaking engagements	Position yourself as an authority; introduce your company indirectly	Cannot directly promote yourself; difficult to measure impact; time consuming	When the audience is relevant	If you're seeking to promote your company or services directly
Word of mouth	Very influential, recommendations are trusted	Difficult to start; difficult to control – could easily turn negative	For products/ services with high involvement purchase decisions or affected by trends and influencers	Fast moving consumer goods
Case studies	Demonstrate benefits that may not immediately be obvious	Many will only scan read; requires a prior interest to get to the point of viewing a case study	Complex purchase decisions such as new products or technology where benefits aren't widely known	Fast moving consumer goods
Crises management	Specialists provide a quick response to any crisis or publicity that could reflect badly on your company; damage control is essential	Need to appoint an agency or specialist in advance of a crisis; can be costly; could be handled incorrectly	Most important for large companies and those working in delicate areas, e.g. fracking, politics	Judged on a case by case basis

01 Purpose
02 Intelligence
03 Proposition
04 Tools
05 Conversion
06 Results

4.0

Tools

Resources – Sales Support/CMS

Also known as traditional marketing methods, these are non-digital tools you can use to reach your customers.

	IN YOUR TOOLKIT			
	Advantages	Disadvantages	When to use	When not to use
Advertising – radio, press, TV, magazines, etc.	Great platform for brand messaging; huge potential audience	Very costly; consumers are overloaded with messages	When you can stand out and convey benefits to a targeted audience	When other avenues get a greater return on investment
Interviews (e.g. with your leaders)	Give insight into your company; position your company as a leader; free publicity	Competitors may be taking note	When your brand is your differentiator	When other avenues prove more time effective

4.0
Tools

IN YOUR TOOLKIT

	Advantages	Disadvantages	When to use	When not to use
Databases (e.g. past customers, website sign ups)	Targeted list of people interested in your company to contact	Be aware of data protection and GPPR laws	Regularly with targeted communications and relevant messages	Too regularly – don't by seen as spammy
Purchased databases	Purchase a targeted list already segmented, e.g. by location	Costly; hit and miss approach; can be seen as annoying; data protection laws heavily restrict how you use databases	When your own data isn't available and other avenues of reaching customers are ineffective	When other avenues are available
Samples and giveaways	Encourage the customer to buy; build engagement	High initial cost; may not lead to future purchase to recoup costs	New product launches	High end and luxury goods – may devalue your offer
Focus groups	Gain valuable feedback from people in your target market	Can delay product launch timescales; large sample size needed for opinions to be representative	For new products or new markets; when you're willing to review and improve	When not relevant to your product or service

01 Purpose
02 Intelligence
03 Proposition
04 Tools
05 Conversion
06 Results

4.0

Tools

	IN YOUR TOOLKIT			
	Advantages	**Disadvantages**	**When to use**	**When not to use**
Partnering with other companies/ services/ products	Piggybacking can align your brand with another that customers like	The other company can also trade off your good brand	When there is a clear connection between the products or services	Where any negative connotations may exist, e.g. if some customers consider the other company/ product unethical
Competitions	Huge potential reach; generate excitement; collect data	Too many can devalue the brand; customers want a prize with high value	To gain attention from new customers; to collect customer data	High end and luxury goods – may devalue your offer
Seasonal campaigns	Great way to get attention and build on existing hype	Lots of competition; can be costly	Follow market trends, e.g. Christmas busy periods, or times relevant to your products/ services	Don't overuse

01 Purpose
02 Intelligence
03 Proposition
04 Tools
05 Conversion
06 Results

4.0
Tools

IN YOUR TOOLKIT				
	Advantages	**Disadvantages**	**When to use**	**When not to use**
Commissioning research	Gain insights; get statistics to use in your marketing	Costly; many variables affect results	Where opinions and statistics will benefit future campaigns	Where data isn't relevant to your market
Sales calls/ telemarketing	Direct conversations with your target market	Difficult or costly to get targeted data; time consuming; data protection laws restrict how you contact people	Most appropriate to certain industries such as energy suppliers	When it will annoy customers or potentially ruin goodwill toward your brand
Sponsorship, e.g. event or TV show sponsorship	Huge potential reach; targeted	Very costly	When the audience is your target market	When other avenues get a greater return on investment
Technical service	Build customer trust; gives added value; encourages repeat purchase	Costly to set up and run; if insufficient resource is available it can reflect negatively	For products that users have questions with, particularly tech	For products and services where technical service is not (or rarely) needed

01 Purpose
02 Intelligence
03 Proposition
04 Tools
05 Conversion
06 Results

4.0
Tools

	Advantages	Disadvantages	When to use	When not to use
IN YOUR TOOLKIT				
Sales promotions and offers	Encourages immediate purchase; added value for customer	Customer may not make a repeat purchase	Where cost is a factor that prevents purchase	For high end or luxury goods/services – this could devalue the perceived worth
Door to door sales	Direct conversations with your target market	Low success rates; can be seen as annoying and untrustworthy; time consuming	Most appropriate to certain industries such as energy suppliers	When it will annoy customers or potentially ruin goodwill toward your brand
Guerrilla marketing (unconventional methods)	Attention grabbing; stands out; easy to share online	Difficult to create something unique that your target audience will appreciate	When it fits with your brand personality	Fast moving consumer goods or products with low involvement purchase decisions

01 Purpose
02 Intelligence
03 Proposition
04 Tools
05 Conversion
06 Results

4.0

Tools

■ Good to know:

In May 2018 the EU introduced new legislation which governs the way businesses hold and use data. This is called the General Data Protection Regulation, or GDPR. In the UK, GDPR is governed by the Information Commissioner's Office (ICO). They provide a wealth of information and resources to help businesses be compliant. Visit their website at https://ico.org.uk

4.0

Tools

Things to consider when choosing your media

The list of tools we've created here isn't exhaustive and you'll likely find new ways to market and promote your business from time to time. All are worth consideration and we've put together these 4 points to help you do a quick analysis of whether each will be useful for your business.

01 Purpose
02 Intelligence
03 Proposition
04 Tools
05 Conversion
06 Results

4.0
Tools

Consider your target audience

We keep going back to customer personas and so should you. They really are your key to understanding the people who buy from you.

Do they engage with the type of media you're looking at?

They may not be on social media but love watching videos online. It's so easy to assume that one group of people behave one way, so another group will behave the same way – but we all know the old saying about what assuming does...

2. Consider your competitors

They may or may not use the same marketing tools. **What does that tell you?** If you hit on a great idea and your customers don't use it, this could be a perfect new way for you to reach people – OR it could be an indication that others have tried it and had no success.

3. Consider your budget

Everything comes down to budget and resources. **Set your budget before you make decisions on which tools to use and make sure you stick to your budget.**

If you're using new tools, it may be wise to trial it and see results before committing to long term plans and expenditure.

4.0

Tools

4. Consider what you want to achieve

You began by creating marketing aims to meet your business objectives.

Do the tools you've chosen help you meet those aims?

We'll look at measuring how much has been achieved in the final section, but if your main aim is to **increase repeat purchases** *yet your marketing tools only target new audiences, there is discord.*

4.0

Tools

Activity: Over to you

It's time to identify the best tools you can choose to create your next marketing campaign.

In the table below, tick the tools you plan to use. In the next column, tick if it aligns to your customer or consumer personas *(this is the acid test: if it doesn't align, why are you using it?).*

In the final column, number the priority:

1. key tools you must use
2. would be beneficial to use
3. use if resources and budget allow

01 Purpose
02 Intelligence
03 Proposition
04 Tools
05 Conversion
06 Results

4.0

Tools

	Will you use this tool?	Does it align with your customer personas?	Priority **1.** highest **2.** useful **3.** if resources allow
BRAND IDENTITY			
Logo and brand consistency			
Brand personality and tone of voice			
Workwear			
Promotional merchandise			

01 Purpose
02 Intelligence
03 Proposition
04 Tools
05 Conversion
06 Results

4.0
Tools

	Will you use this tool? ✓	Does it align with your customer personas? ✓	Priority **1.** highest **2.** useful **3.** if resources allow
DIGITAL MARKETING			
Your website			
Search engine optimisation (SEO)			
Online advertising			
Pay per click (PPC) advertising			
Forums			
Social media			
Email marketing			
Website analytics			
Influencers, bloggers and vloggers			
Content marketing — Blogs			
Content marketing — Videos			
Content marketing — White papers			
Content marketing — Webinars			

4.0

Tools

	Will you use this tool? ✓	Does it align with your customer personas? ✓	Priority **1.** highest **2.** useful **3.** if resources allow
PRINT COLLATERAL			
Sales literature: brochures, posters, flyers, leaflets			
Packaging			
Coupons			
On building and external branding, including vehicle livery			
Pull up banners/ display systems			
Point of sale display (POS)			

01 Purpose
02 Intelligence
03 Proposition
04 Tools
05 Conversion
06 Results

4.0
Tools

	Will you use this tool?	Does it align with your customer personas?	Priority **1.** highest **2.** useful **3.** if resources allow
PUBLIC RELATIONS (PR)			
Press releases			
Events and trade shows			
Speaking engagements			
Word of mouth			
Case studies			
Crises management			

01 Purpose
02 Intelligence
03 Proposition
04 Tools
05 Conversion
06 Results

4.0
Tools

	Will you use this tool?	Does it align with your customer personas?	Priority **1.** highest **2.** useful **3.** if resources allow
RESOURCES – SALES SUPPORT/CMS			
Advertising – radio, press, TV, magazines, etc.			
Interviews (e.g. with your leaders)			
Databases (e.g. past customers, website sign ups)			
Purchased databases			
Networking and attending industry events			
Samples and giveaways			
Focus groups			
Partnering with other companies/services/products			
Competitions			

4.0
Tools

	Will you use this tool?	Does it align with your customer personas?	Priority 1. highest 2. useful 3. if resources allow
RESOURCES – SALES SUPPORT/CMS			
Seasonal campaigns			
Commissioning research			
Sales calls/telemarketing			
Sponsorship, e.g. event or TV show sponsorship			
Technical service			
Sales promotions and offers			
Door to door sales			
Guerrilla marketing (unconventional methods)			

4.0
Tools

Next, think back to the customer journey we looked at in section 1.

How many touchpoints would someone in your target market receive?

4.0
Tools

Tip: be realistic, not everyone will see/hear all the messages you put out.

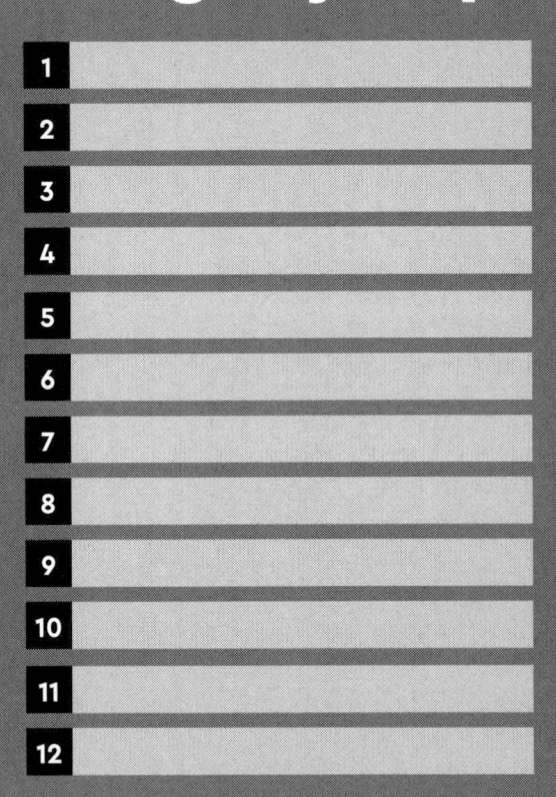

| 1 |
| 2 |
| 3 |
| 4 |
| 5 |
| 6 |
| 7 |
| 8 |
| 9 |
| 10 |
| 11 |
| 12 |

Remember: The average number of touchpoints to convert interest into a sale is 8.

01 Purpose
02 Intelligence
03 Proposition
04 Tools
05 Conversion
06 Results

4.0

Tools

Summary

You should now understand the tools available to you, including:

1 The marketing tools available and their advantages and disadvantages

2 How to choose the right tools for your campaign

3 The variables that will affect the tools you choose

4 Referring back to the customer journey to forecast effectiveness

01 Purpose
02 Intelligence
03 Proposition
04 Tools
05 Conversion
06 Results

05

Conversion

01 Purpose
02 Intelligence
03 Proposition
04 Tools
05 Conversion
06 Results

05
Conversion

"Every contact we have with a customer influences whether or not they'll come back. We have to be great every time or we'll lose them."

Kevin Stirtz, Author

01 Purpose
02 Intelligence
03 Proposition
04 Tools
05 Conversion
06 Results

Conversion

You know your business, your target market and what customers want. You've developed a USP and chosen your marketing tools – excellent!
The next step is to pull this all together to produce your marketing campaign.
To do this, we'll use the Conversion model shown below. It's the perfect blueprint to map our activity into stages to ensure the customer journey is clear, communicated and effective. **In this section we'll look at the stages of conversion:**

1. **Awareness**
2. **Engagement**
3. **Education**
4. **Evaluation**
5. **Sale**
6. **Purchase support**

05

Conversion

Your 'Conversion' Funnel

- AWARENESS
- ENGAGEMENT
- EDUCATION
- EVALUATION
- SALE

01 Purpose
02 Intelligence
03 Proposition
04 Tools
05 Conversion
06 Results

5.0
Conversion

Your 'Conversion' Funnel

The conversion funnel breaks down the process of starting with cold prospects – people who have no prior experience or engagement with your brand – and turning them into paying customers.

The process is shaped like a funnel because the cold prospect starts at the top and the idea is there are 5 steps that buyers go through before they purchase.

For some industries a target audience member may take very little time to move through to the next stage, but all stages still apply.

5.0

Awareness

How to use this model to build a successful campaign

This model maps all of the thinking and intelligence we've developed to date and brings it together so everything happens in the right order, in the right place, at the right time.

The process is shaped like a funnel. The cold prospect starts at the top and the idea is to pull them through the funnel so they emerge a paying customer.

When we've looked at the customer journey previously, this model has served as the base for the theory.

01 Purpose
02 Intelligence
03 Proposition
04 Tools
05 Conversion
06 Results

5.1 Awareness

Awareness

**To become a choice,
you first need to become an option.**

You have a huge target market, and you know there is demand for your products or services because you've done your research. Trouble is, no one has ever heard of you.

The first thing you need to do is generate awareness – that means grabbing the attention of the people in your target market.

This is initial contact, and the first impression your target market will have of your brand. We're not trying to do anything but let them know you exist.

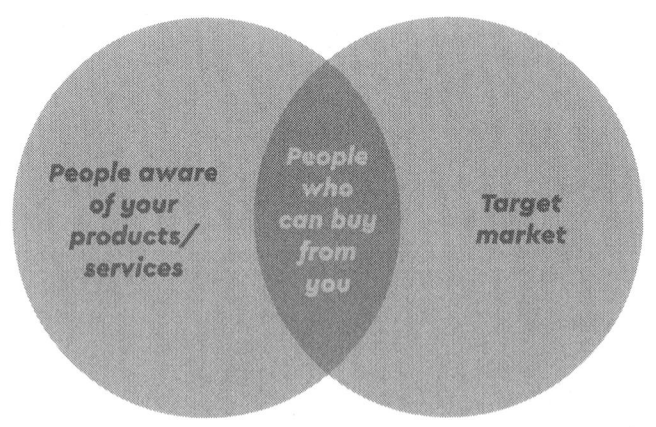

People aware of your products/services

People who can buy from you

Target market

01 Purpose
02 Intelligence
03 Proposition
04 Tools
05 Conversion
06 Results

5.1

Awareness

Methods of generating awareness could include Facebook advertising or attending networking events.

Looking at your chosen marketing tools, which could be the very first contact that makes a person aware of your products or services?

01 Purpose
02 Intelligence
03 Proposition
04 Tools
05 Conversion
06 Results

5.1

Awareness

AWARENESS	Facebook advertising / Website Landing Page / Event / Networking
ENGAGEMENT	
EDUCATION	
EVALUATION	
SALE	

Engagement

When we talk about engagement, we mean people in your target audience engaging with your brand. Engaging could be any kind of communication including commenting on your social media post, phoning your company or speaking to your representative at an event.

The important thing is that they are actively participating in communicating with you.

Which of your marketing tools allow a person to engage with your company?

---

01 Purpose
02 Intelligence
03 Proposition
04 Tools
05 Conversion
06 Results

5.2
Engagement

- **AWARENESS** — Facebook advertising / Website Landing Page / Event / Networking
- **ENGAGEMENT** — Email / Telephone Call / Face-to-Face Meeting
- **EDUCATION**
- **EVALUATION**
- **SALE**

01 Purpose
02 Intelligence
03 Proposition
04 Tools
05 Conversion
06 Results

5.3

Education

Education

Now that the prospect knows about your company and has engaged with it, they need to be educated. Why exactly should they choose you?

This is where you can provide more information to really sell the benefits of what you offer.

Think about the more content-focused tools – including product specs on your website, brochures and content marketing.

Which of your marketing tools educate about the benefits of your offer?

01 Purpose
02 Intelligence
03 Proposition
04 Tools
05 Conversion
06 Results

5.3
Education

AWARENESS — Facebook advertising / Website Landing Page / Event / Networking

ENGAGEMENT — Email / Telephone Call / Face-to-Face Meeting

EDUCATION — Sales Brochure / Info Pack / Free trial / Limited Offer / Webinar / Seminar / Site Visit

EVALUATION

SALE

01 Purpose
02 Intelligence
03 Proposition
04 Tools
05 Conversion
06 Results

5.4

Evaluation

Evaluation

At the evaluation stage, the prospect is weighing up their options.
They're considering if the benefits you offer outweigh what the competition offers.

What's going to tip them over the edge and make you their first choice?

Consider case studies showing how others have benefited, and free content that can be used to persuade them.

Which of your marketing tools persuaded a person who is evaluating their decision?

01 Purpose
02 Intelligence
03 Proposition
04 Tools
05 Conversion
06 Results

5.4
Evaluation

Funnel Stage	Activities
AWARENESS	Facebook advertising / Website Landing Page / Event / Networking
ENGAGEMENT	Email / Telephone Call / Face-to-Face Meeting
EDUCATION	Sales Brochure / Info Pack / Free trial / Limited Offer / Webinar / Seminar / Site Visit
EVALUATION	Social Media Updates / Case Studies / Access to Free Content
SALE	

01 Purpose
02 Intelligence
03 Proposition
04 Tools
05 Conversion
06 Results

5.5

Sale

Sale

We're finally here at the point of sale. The prospect has decided you're the best option to buy from – but before the deal is done, you need to instill confidence they've made the right decision.

What can you do here to make the purchase easier or ensure a smooth sale?

Think about using customer testimonials, offering after sales service and tech support.

Which of your marketing tools seal the deal at the sale stage?

01 Purpose
02 Intelligence
03 Proposition
04 Tools
05 Conversion
06 Results

5.5
Sale

AWARENESS	Facebook advertising / Website Landing Page / Event / Networking
ENGAGEMENT	Email / Telephone Call / Face-to-Face Meeting
EDUCATION	Sales Brochure / Info Pack / Free trial / Limited Offer / Webinar / Seminar / Site Visit
EVALUATION	Social Media Updates / Case Studies / Access to Free Content
SALE	Sales Experience / Customer Testimonial / After Sale Service Plan

5.6
Purchase Support

Purchase Support

This is the hidden item and one that is left forgotten by too many companies. It's not a part of the funnel as it happens after the prospect has become a paying customer, but its importance can make or break companies.

Your marketing shouldn't stop once the customer has purchased from you. Think long term – will a one-off sale help your business survive indefinitely?

Think about repeat purchases, customer loyalty and referrals. Lifelong customers could catapult you from a surviving company to an industry leader.

Purchase support tools could include your after sales support, asking for a testimonial or an email marketing campaign aimed at previous customers.

01 Purpose
02 Intelligence
03 Proposition
04 Tools
05 Conversion
06 Results

5.6
Purchase Support

Tip: **Cross Selling**

This section has links to the education part of the funnel – a customer may be interested in one product but you may be able to educate them on other products you offer.

Cross selling can be very lucrative – would you buy a coffee for £2.40 when you could get a coffee and a cake for £2.60?

Which of your marketing tools offer post-purchase support?

5.6 Purchase Support

Putting it together

Double check that you've listed all of your chosen marketing tools under one of the headings above. It should now be clear when each one comes into play, and the effect it has on someone making a purchase decision.

Placed in order from Awareness to Purchase Support, your tools should now very closely reflect the customer journey and touchpoints you previously identified.
You should be left with an order that is coherent and helps you plan what happens when. The exact timings for your marketing campaign will depend on the industry, product/service and the state of the market.

Think carefully about what you know about the customer and market to plan timescales and assess how long each prospect will spend at each stage of the funnel.

For example, with a high involvement purchase decision the prospect will spend a lot more time at the Education and Evaluation stages than they would for a low involvement purchase decision.

01 Purpose
02 Intelligence
03 Proposition
04 Tools
05 Conversion
06 Results

Purchase Support

Tip: **Hit me baby**

You should have more than 1 tool at each stage of the funnel – remember, not everyone will see all your marketing activity.

5.6

Purchase Support

Tip: Keep Track

Reflect on your previous marketing activity – can you think of tools you've used at every stage above? If not, this could indicate where you've lost prospects along the way.

01 Purpose
02 Intelligence
03 Proposition
04 Tools
05 Conversion
06 Results

5.0

Conversion

Summary

You should now understand how to put your plans together into a campaign. This includes:

1	Why we use our chosen marketing tools

2	Pulling a prospect through each stage of the funnel to emerge a paying customer

3	Reflecting on the customer journey and identifying any missed opportunities

06

Results

01 Purpose
02 Intelligence
03 Proposition
04 Tools
05 Conversion
06 Results

06
Results

"If you can't measure it, you can't improve it."

Peter Drucker, management consultant, educator and author

Keep measuring, keep monitoring

Marketing activity should be a continuous loop of planning, assessing, doing, monitoring, refining and doing some more.

What we're saying is, results don't come at the end of your campaign. Monitoring must happen regularly to allow you to continue planning for the future.

Without looking at your results and refining your activity, marketing can too easily become guesswork and 'this is what we've always done'. **And that's the quickest way to waste money.**

06

Results

It's essential to be proactive and always know where you are so you can plan your next step. Plus, the best type of business intelligence comes from looking at how your target audience have responded to your marketing – and making decisions based on what you know does and doesn't work. **In this section we'll look at:**

1	*Why it's important to measure results*
2	*Different methods of measurement, including digital and traditional media*
3	*How often to review and reflect*
4	*How to evaluate campaign success*

01 Purpose
02 Intelligence
03 Proposition
04 Tools
05 Conversion
06 Results

06
Results

Your 'Results' Model

- Set Your Timeline
- Measure Conversions
- Choose Your Metrics
- **RESULTS**

01 Purpose
02 Intelligence
03 Proposition
04 Tools
05 Conversion
06 Results

6.1
Timeline

Set your timeline 30 / 60 / 90 days

Review, review, review. Your marketing may be planned for the next 6 months, but that doesn't mean you should press Go and leave it alone for that amount of time.

Creating a short, medium and long term timeline helps you align your marketing to your goals and objectives. It gives you focus and allows you to review regularly and make changes to your plan – which means increased effectiveness and more control over your budget.

Are you using a drip or burst campaign, or a mix of both? Regular reviews should indicate whether your strategy is working or if your target market is dropping off before reaching the purchase stage – in which case you can review the Conversion model and make decisions on where improvements need to be made.

01 Purpose
02 Intelligence
03 Proposition
04 Tools
05 Conversion
06 Results

6.2
Conversions

Measure conversions

To measure success, we look at conversions. Conversions come in many forms and tell us that what we're doing has an effect on the customer.

A conversion doesn't necessarily have to be a purchase – it's a way of measuring any improvement within our target market.

For example, if your marketing objective was to increase web traffic by 50%, any awareness you've turned into a website visit counts as a conversion. Success will be determined by whether you've met the 50% target.

Marketing metrics and key performance indicators (KPIs) are measurable values used by sales and marketing teams to demonstrate the effectiveness of campaigns across all marketing channels.
As well as looking at metrics for individual channels, it's important to consider any return on investment (ROI) made.

This involves looking at the total cost for a campaign, and the total profit generated as a result of it. Of course, any effective campaign will have generated more profit than it cost.
There is no definitive figure to aim for – it will vary by industry.

01 Purpose
02 Intelligence
03 Proposition
04 Tools
05 Conversion
06 Results

External factors

To be sure you're analysing your marketing accurately, look for external factors that could affect your metrics – world events, seasonal trends, outside influences and so on.

Tip:
Look at a set time period prior to your campaign and compare these stats against your campaign stats.

6.3
Choose your metrics

Choose your metrics

The best way to measure success is often to choose metrics that demonstrate whether you've achieved your marketing objectives.

We can use measure conversions as follows...

01 Purpose
02 Intelligence
03 Proposition
04 Tools
05 Conversion
06 Results

6.3
Choose your metrics

Awareness

An increase in awareness could be measured in:

1. Website visitor traffic volume
2. Website traffic referrals
3. Inbound links from external sources
4. Amount of positive press and media coverage
5. Media coverage from press – trade and/or consumer
6. Increase in visits to the website/store during a set period of activity
7. Increase in visits to the website during the campaign period

6.3
Choose your metrics

Engagement

Engagement with potential customers could be measured in:

1	Number of enquiries via website contact us / landing pages
2	Number of enquiries via email marketing
3	Number of enquiries via telephone
4	Number of enquiries via face-to-face meetings
5	Number of enquiries via social media activity – LinkedIn/Facebook/Twitter
6	Number of leads gained from events and speaking engagements
7	Number of newsletter sign-ups via website
8	Number of website subscriptions for downloads such as eBooks, whitepapers, How-to Guides, etc.

01 Purpose
02 Intelligence
03 Proposition
04 Tools
05 Conversion
06 Results

6.3
Choose your metrics

Education

Educating potential customers could be measured in:

1	Number of quotations and estimates provided to potential customers
2	Number of plans and specifications created for potential customers
3	Number of face-to-face meetings scheduled following engagement stage
4	Number of telephone conversations scheduled following engagement stage
5	Increase in number of views to website pages with specialist information
6	Number/quality of enquiries via content downloads
7	Number of click-throughs from content marketing
8	Meetings set up from networking and speaking engagements
9	Volume of conversation and replies across a set time period
10	Consumer reply when questioned about exposure to marketing campaign

01 Purpose
02 Intelligence
03 Proposition
04 Tools
05 Conversion
06 Results

6.3

Choose your metrics

Evaluation

1	Number of views of Testimonial website page
2	Amount of traffic from third party review sites such as Trustpilot
3	Number of enquiries coming from referrals
4	Number of discount codes used
5	Number of requests for further information or face-to-face meeting

01 Purpose
02 Intelligence
03 Proposition
04 Tools
05 Conversion
06 Results

6.3

Choose your metrics

Sales

1	Number of sales
2	Average purchase price per customer
3	Increase in revenue during the campaign period (year-on-year)
4	Repeat purchases (loyal customers)
5	Increase in revenue during the campaign period against projections

01 Purpose
02 Intelligence
03 Proposition
04 Tools
05 Conversion
06 Results

6.3
Choose your metrics

Purchase support

1	Calls and emails to customer services
2	Visits to website FAQ page
3	Number of customer referrals

6.3

Choose your metrics

Digital marketing metrics

Digital marketing has opened up so many new avenues to marketers, with unique tools that allow us to measure conversions in new ways.

An overview of some of the tools available is shown next.

01 Purpose
02 Intelligence
03 Proposition
04 Tools
05 Conversion
06 Results

6.3
Choose your metrics

Google Analytics

Google Analytics is a free service offered by Google that generates detailed statistics about the visits to a website. It allows users to review their website's performance including metrics such as:

- Number of visitors (new and returning)
- Location of users
- Which pages have been viewed and for how long
- How long users stayed on the site
- Where users came from (searching for your company/searching for the services you offer/third party referrals)

- What page is being viewed when they close the browser
- Tracked sales
- Tracked products added to basket and their value
- If it's a returning or new user
- Popular days and times of visits
- Bounce rate (when a user visits your site but closes the page fairly quickly without interacting).

This platform will provide vital user data and confirm which pages or products are performing the best across the website. It will also provide insight into how users interact with the website and what the most effective traffic referrals are.

01 Purpose
02 Intelligence
03 Proposition
04 Tools
05 Conversion
06 Results

6.3
Choose your metrics

Social Media

Social media platforms recognise that their networks are of huge value to marketers. The major platforms have introduced tools to plan, analyse and review campaigns – both for paid campaigns and non-paid content.

Facebook has Insights, and Twitter and LinkedIn have their own Analytics sections. These tools automatically monitor activity and allow the user to build custom reports, showing key metrics including page likes, post engagements and website click throughs.

Each post's performance can also be viewed and analysed to allow you to see which types of content – and even the day and time – performs the best with page followers. Better still, many of the platforms will automatically offer suggestions for how to improve engagements and conversions.

Of course, it's down to you as the user to decide which are of value and which are the platform's own marketing, but it's not unusual to see messages pop up for Business Page owners such as 'Your post is performing well. Boost it now to increase click throughs'.

01 Purpose
02 Intelligence
03 Proposition
04 Tools
05 Conversion
06 Results

6.3
Choose your metrics

Social media metrics may include:

1. Number of page likes (overall as well as in a certain time period)
2. Number of comments received/replied to
3. Number of retweets, favourites and direct messages
4. Volume of conversation and replies across a set time period
5. Shares (email is forward to other recipients)

01 Purpose
02 Intelligence
03 Proposition
04 Tools
05 Conversion
06 Results

6.3

Choose your metrics

Email

Email marketing has the massive advantage of being completely measurable, giving great information that can be acted upon.

Metrics available include the number of:

1	Opens

2	Bouncebacks (undeliverable emails)

3	Click throughs

4	Unsubscribes

01 Purpose
02 Intelligence
03 Proposition
04 Tools
05 Conversion
06 Results

6.3
Choose your metrics

But you can also drill down further:

Of those who clicked through, how much time was spent on the site?

Where did those who clicked through look – were they looking at the products/services promoted in the email or something else?

Was a purchase made?

What was their spend?
(Consider spend per user, total spend and average spend)

How many users added items to their basket but didn't complete the purchase?

6.3
Choose your metrics

This intelligence opens up further opportunities – for users who added to their basket but didn't purchase, there is the opportunity to send them a reminder email to complete their purchase, or perhaps a discount code.

Heat maps are also really useful – they allow you to see which points on the email were clicked the most (and least) by showing them as red and green. This is extremely useful as it shows what's important to the reader, and this information can be used to improve future communications.

As well as analysing individual emails, look at the campaign as a whole. What works best in terms of the content? E.g. offers, seasonal content, new product ranges or content marketing such as a new blog release.

You may also choose to look at metrics such as whether open rate increased depending on the day or time the email was received. Many clothing retailers are savvy to shoppers' paydays and are likely to introduce new ranges on or shortly after payday, and send discount codes towards the end of the month when sales start to dip.

6.3
Choose your metrics

Other marketing metrics
CTAs (Call-to-actions)

A call to action is any prompt that encourages a viewer to take any kind of action. For example, on a website it may be a button that says 'Find out more', and on a print advert it may direct the reader to a website or specific landing page.

Call to actions are great because they make the activity measurable.

If you place the same coupon in three magazines, once they're redeemed you won't necessarily know which came from where. But if each coupon has a code relating to the magazine it was published in, you can measure how many came from where – and next time you may choose not to advertise in the one that gave the least results.

01 Purpose
02 Intelligence
03 Proposition
04 Tools
05 Conversion
06 Results

6.3

Choose your metrics

Activity: Measuring the success of your tools

Complete the table on the next page to identify how you will monitor and measure the success of the marketing tools you plan to use.

01 Purpose
02 Intelligence
03 Proposition
04 Tools
05 Conversion
06 Results

6.3

Choose your metrics

Tools you're using	Awareness	Engagement	Education	Evaluation	Sale	Purchase support
Example: press advert with link to landing page	How many people see the ad (circulation)	No. of visits to landing page	No. of people exploring website further/time spent on site		No. of sales originating from the landing page	How many people see the ad (circulation)
Example: social media	No. of page likes (total and this month)	No. of post reactions, click throughs, most popular type of content	No. of questions asked through social media messaging	No. of reviews left and likes/reactions to these	No. of sales tracked from social media, value of these sales	No. of support queries received through social media messaging

NB: most items will not have measurables in every column.

01 Purpose
02 Intelligence
03 Proposition
04 Tools
05 Conversion
06 Results

Evaluating against aims and objectives

You've already planned your marketing tools carefully to fit with your business aims and marketing objectives, so it's safe to say that a successful campaign would mean you are achieving your aims.

Make sure to always refer back to your aims and objectives as these will change as the business and the market evolves.

If your campaign has allowed you to meet some of your marketing objectives but not others, this is a great time to reassess what you could do differently in the future.

6.5
Evaluating against budget

Evaluating against budget

Earlier we showed you how to work out the Return On Investment (ROI) for your campaign as a whole.

If you've only partially met your marketing objectives, it may be useful to work out ROI for each tool you use.

For example, if your aim is to increase sales by 20% this period, and social media has increased sales by 5% but cost you more than the profit you've made, you may make the decision to cut back on the resource allocated.

Tip: When working out ROI remember to include the amount of staff time spent – *employees are a great resource but certainly not a cheap one.*

01 Purpose
02 Intelligence
03 Proposition
04 Tools
05 Conversion
06 Results

06
Results

Summary

You should now understand how, when and why to measure the results of your marketing activity.

This includes:

1 Different methods of measurement, including digital and traditional media

2 How often to monitor and review

3 Reflecting on ROI and evaluating overall campaign success

01 Purpose
02 Intelligence
03 Proposition
04 Tools
05 Conversion
06 Results

THIS ISN'T

The End

IT'S THE **START** OF
SOMETHING AMAZING...

Glossary

Advertising – promoting services with paid audio or visual adverts, for example through TV, radio, press, TV, magazines, etc.

Blog – a regularly updated website or page, usually focusing on one subject and written in an informal or conversational style.

Blogger – someone who writes a blog.

Brand identity – also known as branding, this is the perceived image and subsequent emotional response to a company, its products and services. It allows you to engage with customers and distinguish your company from competitors. Logo, tone of voice, personality and imagery are all part of brand identity.

Burst campaign – a marketing campaign where a lot of activity is delivered in a short space of time, maximising the channels and frequency of messages so customers hear them repeatedly.

Case studies – pieces of writing that detail how a product or service has been used to the benefit of a previous customer, with the hope of persuading the reader to purchase.

Content marketing – creating and sharing material that is of interest to a certain audience, with the aim not to make an immediate sale but to be informative and be seen as a credible source of information.

Coupons – in addition to traditional printed vouches, online coupons and discount codes are rapidly gaining popularity.

Crises management – the process used by a company to manage PR when a disruptive and unexpected event occurs. A PR tool used to limit and minimise negative reaction.

Databases – a marketing database holds personal data on many people, who may or may not be customers.

Digital marketing – this includes any marketing activity that consumers can see online – including on their mobiles.

Display system – also known as an exhibition stand, these are branded and used at events as a form of branding.

Door to door sales – also known as canvassing, this involves a salesperson knocking on people's doors to sell or advertise a product or service.

Drip campaign – a marketing campaign where activity is spread out over a long period of time, allowing the customer continually hear about what you have to offer.

Email marketing – sending emails, usually in very large quantities, with the aim of promoting products or services. Emails are often highly targeted according to the receiver's demographics or preferences.

Focus group – a group of people in a target market brought together to discuss a product to provide feedback, with the aim of the company making improvements before the product is launched.

Forum – a place online where people can discuss particular subjects with other people at the same time.

Guerrilla marketing – using unconventional methods to promote products or services in a way that stand out because they are so different to the usual channels used.

Influencer – a person with credibility in a specific field who often has a large amount of followers online, and so can influence large audiences with their opinions and reach.

Networking – developing relationships with new contacts, traditionally done at networking events but more often being done online and with the aid of social media.

Online advertising – an advert that uses the internet to deliver its message, such as banner advertising, pop ups and social media advertising.

Glossary

Pay per click (PPC) advertising – online advertising that charges the advertiser based on the number of clicks from viewers, including Google Ads and social media advertising.

Point of sale display (POS) – a type of promotion found at or near the physical point of sale, such as at a till in a supermarket.

Press release – a statement written by a company and distributed to news agencies to share a newsworthy story, in the hope of gaining press coverage.

Print advertising – any type of advertising in print material such as newspapers, magazines, brochures and leaflets.

Promotional merchandise – branded items to promote your company, such as pens and notepads. Usually given away free.

Public relations (PR) – the practice of managing the spread of information between an individual or an organisation and the public. The activity is usually free (though you may pay an agency to manage it).

Pull up banner – a retractable banner used to display company branding and information. Often used at exhibitions and events.

Route to market – the way your customers purchase your product. Examples include direct selling, selling in a shop, selling wholesale, distance selling and online selling.

Sales literature – any printed material designed to encourage a sale, including brochures, posters, flyers and leaflets.

Sales promotions – offers given to encourage a sale, such as 50% off and buy one get one free.

Search engine optimisation (SEO) – a series of alterations made to a website or web page that allows search engines to clearly read it, with the intention of the website being placed higher in search engine results and so more easily found.

Seasonal campaigns – marketing activity with messaging that revolves around a seasonal activity, such as Christmas or Easter.

Social media – websites and applications that enable users to create and share content or to participate in social networking.

Sponsorship – the paid practice of partnering with an event, TV show or other medium to gain maximum brand exposure.

Technical service – offering support to customers, usually by phone or internet, to offer advice and assistance on how to use a product or service.

Telemarketing – also known as sales calls, this involves placing outgoing calls with the aim to sell products or services.

Trade show – an exhibition or event aimed at a certain industry, designed to give companies the opportunity to showcase their products and services, network and meet potential partners and customers.

Vlogger – someone who creates vlogs – a video version of a blog.

Webinar – a seminar conducted over the internet.

Website analytics – the collection and measurement of metrics for a certain website, used to analyse and report on how the site is being used.

White paper – a detailed report giving information or proposals on an issue or development, often used by companies to position themselves as an authority on the topic.

Word of mouth – the passing of information from person to person by oral communication. Encouraged by companies who want to get their target audience talking (favourably) about their products or services.

*Source Reference

Page 12 – Coca Cola – Missions, vision and values   www.coca-cola.co.uk/about-us/mission-vision-and-values

Page 12 – BMW Group – Core values   www.bmwgroup.jobs/us/en/culture.html

Page 14 – Schultz, H. "Pour Your Heart Into It: How Starbucks Built a Company One Cup at a Time" by Howard Schultz, Dori Jones Yang (1997)

Page 19 – KitKat, Nestle Group   www.kitkat.co.uk/content/

Page 19 – Loreal Paris   www.loreal-paris.co.uk/

Page 19 – HSBC Holdings   https://www.hsbc.co.uk/

Page 30 – Google   www.about.google/

Page 30 – Facebook   www.facebook.com/notes/mark-zuckerberg/bringing-the-world-closer-together/10154944663901634/

Page 100 – SWOT Analysis Model, Humphrey, A. (1960)

Page 120 – Virgin Holidays, 'Holiday like a rockstar' advertising campaign (2011)   www.virginholidays.co.uk/

Page 124 – Domino's Pizza   www.dominos.com.sg/CorporateInformation/Unique

Page 124 – FedEx Corporation – Unique Selling Proposition 1978 – 1983 – www.forbes.com/pictures/egdi45gded/federal-express-when/#37a021d2268c   www.fedex.com

Page 124 – AVIS – 'We're number two. We try harder' advertising campaign 1962   www.avis.co.uk

Notes

Notes

marketingskills academy

Copyright © 2022 by Simon Clayton, Marketing Skills Academy.

All rights reserved. No part of this publication may be reproduced, distributed, or transmitted in any form or by any means, including photocopying, recording, or other electronic or mechanical methods, without the prior written permission of the publisher, except in the case of brief quotations embodied in critical reviews and certain other noncommercial uses permitted by copyright law. For permission requests, please email the publisher, addressed "Attention: Permissions Coordinator," to simon@marketingskillsacademy.co.uk or tel: 01642 688678.

Marketing Skills Academy is a registered trading name for Elevation Marketing Limited.
Registered in England & Wales No. 9163358.

Ordering Information: Quantity sales - special discounts are available on quantity purchases by corporations, associations, and others. For details, contact the publisher at the address above.
Published in the United Kingdom.

www.marketingskillsacademy.co.uk

Printed in Great Britain
by Amazon